THE DEFINING MOMENT

Leonard Renier

Wealth & Wisdom, Inc.
www.WealthandWisdominc.com

ISBN 0-7414-5220-0

Published by:

PUBLISHING.COM

1094 New DeHaven Street, Suite 100
West Conshohocken, PA 19428-2713
Info@buybooksontheweb.com
www.buybooksontheweb.com
Toll-free (877) BUY BOOK
Local Phone (610) 941-9999
Fax (610) 941-9959

Printed in the United States of America

Printed on Recycled Paper

Published February 2009

ACKNOWLEDGMENTS

There are people who have influenced my life and my way of thinking, who have helped me find the energy to write my opinions. My wife, Janice, with her love and support, is the center of my life. She gave me encouragement to complete this task. My children – Jacqui, Colleen, Beth, and Zeb – are with me every day in my heart and mind.

The people who expanded my knowledge in my business played an important role in my life. Don Blanton, founder of Money Trax, Inc., changed my career. His knowledge runs parallel with many of my thoughts. Much of my passion comes from the professionals across the country who I've been fortunate to meet. They are committed and dedicated, and are a tremendous source of knowledge.

At the office, Felicia Hull fights the daily battle of keeping things glued together and running well. Her support is sometimes my only sanctuary. Nothing can replace the nice things that she and all the other members of our office have done for me.

CONTENTS

Foreword

The guarantees in life are limited to what we know, so it only makes sense to know as much as we possibly can. I have been in the financial services business for more than forty years, and I have seen and lived through financial trends, both up and down. The key factor that has remained the same for successful people in both the good and bad times is their ability to adjust to situations by using logic, knowledge, and common sense.

Unfortunately, many people don't get opportunities to learn how money works. Knowing how money works is a great thing. Not knowing can be disastrous. In light of all the economic changes and challenges, there has never been a more important moment in preparing for our future.

A few years ago, I met Leonard Renier who had recently founded Wealth & Wisdom Institute. He expressed deep concern about the direction we were heading as a country and the impact it would have on everyone. Since then, a growing group of professionals from across the country have dedicated themselves to educating people and helping them prepare for the future we are all facing. I am proud to serve on the institute's President's Advisory Council. Today, many professionals have joined together to help individuals

1

realize the financial potential in their lives. It is my shared hope, with Len, that you too will experience the Defining Moment that will change your life.

Leroy Lopez

San Diego, California

The Defining Moment

The Opening

When it comes to history, we are only here for a brief moment. Most people will go through life having some impact on the coming generations of our society. In my profession, I have chosen a path that will change lives now, and for the next generation. I believe I have an obligation to make people aware of options and opportunities that they might have. My intent is to deliver more information and more knowledge so that people can make better financial decisions. You see, people cannot be aware of something that they are not aware of. How can a person say "yes" or "no" to an opportunity that they don't even know exists?

For many people, their current economic situation is a matter of choice, not a matter of chance. Many decisions they make are misguided and self-inflicted, and these decisions are made with a limited amount of knowledge. Some decisions were made in fear and many people are cautious of change, so financial decisions, on many occasions, are made by default, without knowledge and unaware of future unintended consequences that they may create.

Today, many Americans need to hear that they are not the only ones that are confused about everyday financial situations. They want to talk to someone who can communicate and explain logically what is going on. They want a better understanding of how their decisions of today will impact their everyday lives and their future. Many Americans are also looking for an organized method, a thought process that will create a defining moment in the way they think about money. It is my intent that in the pages of this book, that with more information and more knowledge, the reader will have the ability to make better life decisions. This book may create a lot of questions in your mind, but that is a good thing; it tells me you are beginning to think, instead of being told what to think. Today, many Americans are involved in the evolution of transferring their wealth away to those who: 1. Create the situations; 2. Control the outcomes; and 3. Profit from it. This is a vicious cycle that needs to end.

I have joined a growing group of professionals from across the country who are deeply concerned about the direction we are headed as a nation and the impact it will have on everyone's financial future. This information is so critical to your future that I feel I have an obligation to share it with you. First, you must come to an understanding of how current economic and demographic conditions will impact your everyday life, and then learn a logical approach to gain control of your personal finances. I will explain to you some of the problems we will be facing in the future, uncover some financial myths, and give you a greater understanding of how to recapture and keep money that you are unknowingly and unnecessarily transferring or giving away.

It is not my intent to scare or alarm anyone, but to issue a wakeup call to get readers to pay attention and address the problems we face as a nation and in our personal lives, before it becomes a crisis.

In the Beginning...

Waking up in the morning, for most of us, is a real treat when considering the alternative. For those of us who are thirty-five years old or older, I am a little surprised that we have managed to survive at all.

Some of us were born relatively normal even though our mothers may have occasionally smoked cigarettes and drank alcohol during pregnancy. Then as folklore has it, after nine months of incubation, we were greeted with a slap on our backside by the first stranger we saw. Welcome to the real world. Surviving the trauma of birth was fairly easy, compared to being laid face down in a brightly colored crib coated in lead-based paint, surrounded by soft covers, stuffed animals, and small bite-sized playthings that could unintentionally suffocate any one of us. Growing up was exciting. Our parents drove us around in cars with no car seats, seat belts, padded dashes, or airbags. As kids, we were not protected by childproof medicine bottles, childproof doors, cabinets, stairways, or childproof electrical wall outlets. We grew up riding bikes with no helmets and had the courage to drink water from faucets and occasionally directly from a water hose. We shared soft drinks with our friends from the same bottle and just about everything we ate was made with butter and lots of sugar. We would go outside and play all day. We did not have Game Boys, Nintendo, Xboxes, or video games. We did not have cable TV with 150 channels, video movies or DVDs, surround sound, cell phones, computers or Internet chat rooms, let alone iPods.

We would go outside and find our friends. We played. We fell out of trees, got bruised, and cut and bumped our heads, and there were no lawsuits from these injuries. We played with sticks, BB guns, dart guns, bows and arrows, and played dodge ball and tackle football with no equipment on. We tried out for sports teams and Little League, and not everyone made the team. Those who did not make it had to deal with the disappointment. In school, we could actually fail a grade and be held back a year or two. We would hitchhike from place to place, and if we ever got in trouble or broke the law, our parents actually sided with the law and punished us more. There was discipline and responsibility in our lives. Somehow, we all survived.

As a testimony to our ability to adapt to situations, our generation produced some of the best risk takers, problem solvers, and inventors in history. Growing up, we learned to analyze situations, applying information and knowledge that was available at the time, which would help us predict outcomes and see opportunities logically. In the past 50 years, there has been an explosion of innovation and ideas. We have experienced freedom, failure, success, and responsi-bility. We learn how to deal with it all. It is here, in these lessons of life, where we formed our decision-making process.

Paying Attention

I would like to thank my grade-school teachers for the very first lessons of life that were instilled into me. Their life lesson was very clear and to the point: Leonard, pay attention...concentrate. At the time, it was a sobering warning that usually interrupted some sort of daydreaming. But, looking back, if applied to one's life, it is one of the most important lessons we can use in our daily lives. Paying attention is difficult to do, especially if the topic is dull and boring. Although these topics are important in our lives, many times we take the "yeah, whatever" attitude in trying to understand them. Most of life's follies, mistakes, and accidents are caused because we are not paying attention to what is going on around us. Mistakes and accidents cost money. In many aspects of our daily lives, the lack of concentration and attention to the details of our everyday financial lives costs us dearly.

It took a long time for the lesson from grade school of "paying attention" to take hold. That is because we are fed a consistent message that taking control of our financial lives will be fairly easy, and others will help us do it, no problem. The others I refer to are planners, banks, investment people, and the government. Unfortunately the focus of these groups, and they are very focused, is to profit from you.

What is needed to avoid unintended cones-quences is a thought process. Many people transfer away much of their wealth unknowingly and unnecessarily. It is no surprise that very few people know how money works, and when you do not understand something, it is difficult to concentrate on it. Over a period of time, if you do not pay attention to even a simple thought process, it becomes forgotten. The problem is, many people have not been taught a process, and they must rely on others to pay attention for them. This could be a big mistake.

In developing a thought process to help you think through financial situations, you may reduce or eliminate mistakes and accidents in the future. To help you with this thought process, I will share with you the Ten Defining Moments. Conceptually, you need to see ideas from a different perspective. The Ten Defining Moments will become a guide for you in the way you approach your financial future. This is a thought process, not a list of recommended products. The Ten Defining Moments is an understanding of how money works.

Insecure Security

The recent study by the Rockefeller Foundations on the American Worker Economic Security Survey reported that:

- Americans would prefer economic security to higher pay;
- Eighty percent of Americans would prefer a secure pension or health care over a guaranteed job;

- Americans believe things have gotten less secure;
- They also expect things to get less secure;
- Many lack health care;
- Pension coverage is stagnant;
- Personal savings rates have plummeted;
- Half of the people feel they lack enough savings to weather a crisis;
- Most feel they are not saving enough for retirement; and
- Nearly half worry about Social Security cutbacks.

The conclusion of the report shows Americans are deeply concerned about their financial security. These are serious problems.

David Walker, the former Comptroller General of the United States, stated, *"The United States may be the greatest nation in history, but we rely too much on our temporary sole superpower status and our past successful track record. Too many Americans are living for today rather than taking steps to prepare a better tomorrow. America is suffering from tunnel vision, short sightedness, and self-centeredness."* He goes on to say that America is not taking the challenges seriously enough. This must change for the sake of our country, our children, and our grandchildren. A history lesson may prod us to act sooner than later when addressing America's problems. The Roman Republic lasted over 500 years, but it fell for several reasons − three of which seem to resonate today. First, a decline in moral values and political civility at home. Second, an overconfident and over-intended military around the world. Third, fiscal irresponsibility by the central government. These are reasons great nations failed.

Americans continue to spend more money than they make. They are going deeper into debt, paying the price of compounding interest and facing a future where they will have trouble making the minimum payments on their personal debt. For the first time since 1934, Americans have spent more money than they have taken home. This alone creates everyday insecurity.

Competition

Without competition, we would still be living in caves.

In many cases, we have priced ourselves out of the world marketplace.

The American public sets the acceptable price for products – competition sets the quality within that pricing structure.

It will be difficult in the global marketplace to compete in profitability and quality when we are competing with a $6.00–$8.00 labor force.

Guilt-tripping us into buying American products simply because it will impact a worker's retirement benefit is a bad marketing ploy.

In the coming years, India will have twice as many honor students as we have students. China will have twice as many honor students as India.

How will we compete in this changing world economy?

The government itself has "regulated" us out of some markets in which we use to prosper. Shipping, the oil industry, cruise lines, household items, TVs, clothing, etc. have gone the way of imports due to taxes, government regulations, and cheaper labor costs.

When it comes to the global economy, the world needs us. We are a consumer nation. We do one thing well: We buy stuff. As the world economy creates more consumers, it will not have to rely just on America to buy their goods.

How many more industries here at home must we sacrifice to the world economy? How long can we compete with a $20 an hour labor force when we are against countries that will compete paying only half of that amount?

A Billion What?

When it comes to government high finance, I think we need to slow down and pay attention. Our government representatives throw the billion word around like they own a forest full of money trees. What kind of tree are you? What is a billion? Well, about a billion seconds ago, it was 1959. A billion minutes ago, Jesus was walking around. A billion hours ago was the

Stone Age, and a billion days ago, no one walked around on the earth on two feet. How does our government view a billion? Well, a billion dollars ago was eight hours and 20 minutes ago. To put things into perspective, let's look at the flooding of New Orleans. The senator from that area was asking the Federal Government for $250 billion dollars to rebuild the city. If you were one of the 484,674 residents (every man, woman, and child), you would each get $516,528. Or, if you are talking about 188,251 homes there, that represents $1,329,787 per house. So, that means if you were a family of four, your family's share of the money requested by the senator would be $2,066,012. Is anyone paying attention? One might conclude that the only power a government representative has is their ability to spend our money.

A Professional
Services Business

Many professionals in the financial services business have the luxury of not knowing what they *should* know. You see, they cannot be aware of something they are not aware of. Some professionals in this industry have it all wrong. It is about the people, not the company's product of the month, or their ranking in a sales contest. Many times the public can become confused between what is good sound advice and someone's desire to be recognized by a company for their sales activity. From a distance, you can see the dilemma that the public must deal with. In every aspect of their lives, from the media, left and right wing politics, and even some religions, people are being told *what* to think, not how and why to think. This has a paralyzing effect on the average person's ability to make necessary life decisions. Information and a decision-making thought process are required to make such decisions. Knowledge does not become wisdom simply because it is repeated over and over again until it is accepted as "the only truth." Knowledge can be memorized, but wisdom is the art of applying knowledge to one's life. Without a process or a guide in your decision-making, recognizing the difference between opportunity and a company's sales goals will be difficult.

Defining Moment #1

Your money will never be worth more than it is today.

Every financial institution understands the power of money. They also understand the term: "the velocity of money." Money that doesn't move or have velocity is like money that is stuffed in a mattress: It doesn't create wealth or profits. To give you an example, the average bank in the United States spends a dollar about five and a half times. They take money, and it is not even their money, that is deposited in their bank and lend it to other people. These people, who borrowed the money, make payments back to the bank and pay interest. The bank then takes those monthly payments and lends that money out again, over and over. This process continues repetitively about five times on each dollar they touch. This is very profitable for the bank just in collecting interest in this process. But, they understand one rule that creates more profit for them than just collecting interest: They understand that MONEY WILL NEVER BE WORTH MORE THAN IT IS TODAY. Due to inflation, the buying power of a dollar decreases over time. The buying power of $1,000 today with a 3% inflation factor built in will have the buying power of only $412 in 30 years. The banks and lending institutions understand this clearly. They may even encourage you to make additional monthly payments on the money they lent you. The banks are in a win-win situation. If you don't make additional payments, they will collect more interest over time. If you do make additional payments, they will take that money and spend it five and a half times, thus increasing their profits. Money will never be worth more than it is today.

If we apply this defining moment to our everyday lives, the lesson becomes more apparent. According to the Government Accountability Office (GAO) and David Walker, the former Comptroller General of the United States, American households have spent more money than they took home the first time since 1934, during the Great Depression. The average American's ability to hang on to today's money, which has the most buying power now, is being sent to someone else in the form of debt payments. A greater number of Americans are becoming more deeply concerned about the increasing costs of health care, housing, taxes, energy costs, and rising college tuition for their children. The average American finds themselves in the dilemma of caring for their children and caring for their aging parents. The ability for Americans to save "today's" dollars has all but diminished. The traditional approach to family financial affairs cannot continue down the same path. It must change, and the sooner, the better. What is really needed is more financial literacy. Our government should not be expected to take an active role in addressing family fiscal problems. Typically, the government does not respond to problems until they reach crisis proportions.

Understanding that your money will never be worth more than it is today is a defining moment in itself and it will impact the other nine defining moments that we will discuss. But alone, by itself, let's talk about this and how it may impact your thought process in your everyday life.

Inflation

I remember when I was youngster pulling into a gas station in my two-ton 1959 Ford and purchasing gas for 19 cents a gallon. If that is not amazing enough, an attendant would come out and pump the gas for me, check my oil, clean my windshield, and then politely thank me for my two-dollar purchase. There is a lesson there. Not only has inflation adjusted the price of things we purchase today, but also on a second front, it has diminished customer service, professionalism, and direct customer contact. Our society changed in the 1960s, and we created a whole generation of "what's in it for me" and "I want it now" folks. Companies marketing to this group focused on "making it faster" and "making it cheaper." In the '70s, we lived the lesson of inflation firsthand. Mortgage and interest rates skyrocketed into the 20% range and political leadership declined. We learned the hard way that inflation had a direct correlation to our future dollar's buying power. Unfortunately this caused more Americans at that time to become more dependent on government programs, and this created another cycle of costs that was passed on to the taxpayer. What we must understand is that inflation is a double-edged sword. It creates higher prices (less buying power per dollar) and fewer services (you pumping your own gas).

Let's take a look at an example of how inflation can eat away at your buying power. A thousand dollars today with a three percent inflation rate calculated per year will have only $744 dollars of buying power in ten years. This means you would need $1,343 in ten years to have the same buying power of $1,000 today. In 20 years at 3% inflation, that $1,000 would have only $553 of buying power and in 30 years only $412. In that 30th year, you will need $2,427 to have the same buying power as $1,000 today. Inflation should be an informed concern of every American because it will impact their everyday lives.

We should also be concerned about inflation at another level. The debit level of the Federal Government is in the ten trillion-dollar range. At current interest rates, the government is paying about $41 million dollars an hour just in interest on its debt. That is $690,000 a minute, $11,500 per second, just in interest. Most of this debt is owned by foreign nations, and if interest rates go up, as a country, we are in trouble. David Walker, the former Comptroller General of the United States, alluded to this on his website and said, "The United States is on a burning platform with no exit strategies." He went on to say, "The status quo is not an option. We face large and growing structural deficits largely due to known demographic trends. To balance the government budget by 2040 may require cutting the total federal budget by 60% or raising federal taxes to two times today's level."[1] Neither of these is a good option, and either will undoubtedly direct more of your future dollars away from you and your family, and more toward the Federal Government.

---

[1] David Walker, 6/30/07.

If you own a home and have a mortgage on it, you are probably the proud recipient of a lot of junk mail. Much of this mail is from financial institutions that want to inform you that making additional payments on your mortgage is a good thing. For whom it is a good thing is not clear. So, let me ask you one question: Would you like to make more house payments now with dollars that will never be worth more than they are today? If your mortgage payment is $1,000 per month, do you want make more payments now when your money has the buying power of $1,000, or make more payments thirty years from now when the buying power of that money is $412 ($1,000, 3% inflation rate for 30 years)? What you need to understand is that the value of your home is going to go up or down, no matter what your monthly payment is. I want to live in the nicest house I can, with the least amount of monthly payment in today's dollars. By making additional payments or paying cash up front for my house, I have used the most expensive dollars I could to do this. At the same time, by using today's money to make additional payments, I have made the banks and mortgage companies very happy. Remember, they are in a win-win situation.

SEM

There may be times in our lives when it would make sense to fund the things we want with someone else's money (SEM), i.e. banks, credit card companies, mortgage companies, financial institutions. We do this all the time with our homes, cars, and education costs. The reality is that if we do this, we are going to have to pay a premium (interest) to someone for the use of their money. There are good ways, and there are bad ways to use someone else's money in your life. For many Americans, it has become too easy to use someone else's money for the wrong reasons. Today, some Americans are drowning in monthly payments for the luxury of using this type of money. I do see a purpose for using someone else's money (SEM) when it involves reasonable interest rates, a long-term commitment, and a hard asset, such as a house or other real estate, as collateral.

Velocity of Money

If you were to dig a hole in your backyard, bury ten thousand dollars in it, and cover it up, what would happen? Ten years later, you could dig it up and you would still have ten thousand dollars in currency, but that money would have less buying power than it had ten years ago. Money sitting still by itself, with no movement, gains nothing. *Velocity of Money* should also not be confused with investing money, let's say in stocks, bonds, or mutual funds. In investing, the hope is that your money will increase in volume. If you continually get positive rates of return from investing in the market, that growth in your money could offset the decreasing buying power and taxes that you will be facing in the future. It is always good to remember that in investing, the only person at risk of losing is you. You will always be approached by people promising you higher rates of return. Ask yourself, who's at risk: you or the person making the recommendations?

So, what is the *Velocity of Money*? Let's use an example of a bank. As I mentioned before, a bank will spend one dollar about five and a half times. They will take money from savings accounts and CDs and lend that money to someone else. The person who borrowed the money pays the bank back plus interest. The bank takes that payment they received from that loan and they lend it to someone else. Now the bank has two monthly payments coming in, plus interest, and they lend that money out again. This process goes on about five and one half times. They have created the *Velocity of Money* that can cycle a dollar through this process many times. We need to pay attention to the fact that the banks have accomplished this feat without using any of their money but rather by using the money that we deposited in their bank.

By understanding how a bank creates the velocity of money, it becomes clear why banks and lending institutions urge you to make additional monthly payments. These businesses understand one thing: Money will never be worth more than it is today (buying power), and the faster money comes in, the faster they can spend it five and a half times. Much of the marketing from these companies emphasizes the importance of paying off your loans as soon as you can. Everyone would love to be debt free, but at what cost to our buying power? The banks and lending institutions clearly understand that money will never be worth more than it is today due to inflation, and the velocity of money creates wealth for them. They are in a win-win situation. They can collect money from you via extra or additional loan payments and spend that money faster, or collect interest and principle payments as they come due. Having the ability to spend a dollar more than once is the definition of velocity of money. Once again, this is different than getting a rate of return on your money.

In my travels across the country, I have had the opportunity to discuss "the velocity of money" with thousands of people. As always, the goal of these discussions is to encourage people to think, not simply to be told what to think. Being told what to think is devoid of ideas and creativity. Many times, I like to engage people in things that they need to understand, so I walk them through a lesson in life and the velocity of money.

If I am addressing a group of people, I will ask someone to lend me twenty dollars. Someone is always kind enough to oblige me, and I tell the rest of the people to get out their wallets and purses because we are going to play an exciting game. I will hold up the twenty dollars I have just borrowed and sell it to the first person who can give me a ten-dollar bill. This exchange usually happens rather quickly. I ask the person who just purchased a twenty-dollar bill for a ten, "How do you feel?" Their response is usually favorable. Now I am holding a ten-dollar bill, and I say I would like to sell the ten dollars for a five-dollar bill. This trade also takes little or no time to accomplish. I ask that person how they feel. They typically feel pretty good also. Now I want to sell the five-dollar bill I have from that transaction for a one-dollar bill. This happens quickly because everyone is beginning to learn how the game works. I am left holding a one-dollar bill, and I ask, "Now that you know how to play the game, I have a pocketful of twenty-dollar bills, do you want to play again?" Of course, everyone wants to play again because now they understand how to play the game. I take the one-dollar bill I have left and return it to the person I borrowed the twenty dollars from and ask them how they feel. Not so good, right? I note that I gained three new friends at the expense of one. Now I ask, "Where is our big winner?" Usually the person who bought the twenty dollars for ten dollars jumps up. Wrong! You see, that person did well but only doubled his money. The person who paid one dollar for five dollars did much better: They got five times what they paid out.

What is more important in this lesson is that three people learned how it felt to be the bank, buying and selling money. They all felt pretty good and made good money. They all realized it was easy to do once they knew how to do it. They all wanted to be in the banking business now. On the surface, they all understood the lesson I presented, but I need to take them a layer deeper in their thought process. What is really going on is that the banks and lending institutions are distributing thirty-five dollars (a twenty, a ten, and a five) for nineteen dollars (twenty dollars borrowed and had one dollar left), and they are collecting interest on the thirty-five dollars from the twenty dollars that was not theirs in the first place. They have created something out of nothing. The velocity of money and interest collected pays for the nineteen dollars they borrowed and much, much more. Every dollar collected by a bank has a future value attached to it.

Unfortunately, most of us are caught up in the other side of their game of paying interest. Unknowingly, many people are so caught up in debt and interest payments that it is ruining their lives. Their ability to use "today's" dollars that have the most buying power is gone because those dollars are going to someone else.

LUC

Another aspect of this lesson is that the people who had Liquidity, Use, and Control (LUC) of their money were able to take advantage of an opportunity when it came along. They had the money to buy the twenty dollars for ten; ten dollars for five, and the five dollars for one. All too often, people have all their money tied up in other areas. They have prepaid this or overfunded that, to a point where if they need money for a real opportunity, they can't get to their money. Ask yourself a question, "How often does opportunity knock, and how long will it wait for you?"

LOC

As for the poor person I borrowed the twenty dollars from, he suffered a "lost opportunity cost." Not only did he lose nineteen of today's dollars but also the ability to earn money from the nineteen dollars, forever. On a daily basis, many people give away a lot of their money unknowingly and unnecessarily. This problem is compounded when they also lose the ability to earn money on that money, which negates any opportunity to create velocity of money.

Defining Moment #2

This may be the lowest tax bracket you will ever be in.

"We are heading for a future where we will have to double federal taxes or cut federal spending by 60%."

David Walker, former Comptroller General of The United States

The rapidly changing demographics of our country are going to impact everyone's lives in our nation. It can no longer be expected that the United States can dictate, from the pulpit, the direction and course of the world as a whole. Simply believing we are a great nation will not continue to make us one. To compete and survive, we will have to change and that change may not come easy. We may have to rid ourselves of some of our contempt, political self-righteousness, and the need to blame someone for our lack of competition in a global economy. Although the United States will remain a powerful nation, our ability to change will be our measuring stick in the future.

"As a nation we have already made promises to coming generations of retirees that we will be unable to fulfill."

Alan Greenspan

As you are reading these words, the U.S. Federal Government is continuing to spend $1.35 for every dollar it takes in from tax revenues. The debit in our nation is growing at forty-one million dollars an hour, six hundred and ninety thousand dollars a minute, and that is just on the interest on that debt. According to the Government Accountability Office (GAO), the Federal Government fiscal burden in the year 2000 was twenty point four (20.4) trillion dollars. Today, that burden has expanded to over fifty (50.0) trillion dollars. What does that mean to every person in the United States? Well, in order to pay for this government burden, every person in the country would have to pay more than $156,000. For every full-time worker, that comes to around $375,000, or for every household $411,000. The purpose of telling you this is not to scare you, but rather to make you aware that all the conditions are in place for everyone's taxes to increase. Traditional-thinking professionals may be willing to avoid this problem that is out there right now until it becomes a crisis for you. Then it is simply too late to react to the problem.

Future taxes that you pay will be one of the largest transfers of your money that you will ever make. The size and amount of future taxes has not yet been determined, but we do know that government debt will be a large determining factor. Another issue in the future tax equation is that the labor force in the United States will continue to decline. We already know that from a percentage standpoint, there will be fewer taxpaying workers than there are retirees who are and will be on government programs (Social Security, Medicare, Medicaid, etc.) and they will be living longer.

So, let's do the math. We have a declining workforce in the United States. We have an aging population living longer on government programs. We have a government that spends $1.35 for every dollar of revenue they take in. We have over $50 trillion dollars in future government fiscal burdens. Unfortunately, the only source of revenue for the Federal Government comes from collecting taxes. From the government's standpoint, do you think they are going to lower taxes or raise taxes and/or decrease government benefits?

"Closing the long-term fiscal gap would require real average annual economic growth in the double-digit range every year for the next 75 years. The U.S. economy grew an average 3.2 percent in the 1990s."

David Walker, former Comptroller General of The United States

Imagine now, if you can, your future savings and retirement money being taxed at two times today's levels. Once again, this is an estimate from the government's GAO. Traditional thinkers and the so-called experts from the government are now telling us that in order to survive in the future, where we will all be living longer, we must save more money now. I imagine if I could spend $1.35 for every dollar I get, like the government does, I'd be okay. But, I can't. From the government's own study, it reveals that the personal savings rate in the U.S. has declined. In fact, this is the lowest amount of personal savings recorded since 1934, during the Great Depression. The idea of someone saving more now, so they can pay higher taxes in the future is a game I do not necessarily want to play.

You may experience a defining moment in your thinking by answering this question: If given a choice, would you want to receive money now, when taxes are the lowest, or later when taxes may be much higher? If you are successful and are saving money and deferring the taxes to a later date, you may want to rethink the dilemma awaiting you. The old adage: "You will probably retire to two-thirds of your income, thus be in a lower tax bracket" may be floating around in your mind. Think! That thought is saying: I want less money, so I don't have to pay as much in taxes. That is not a great solution, but that comment has become so commonplace in traditional thinking it somehow magically became acceptable. Do you want to retire with the least amount of money, or the most?

"We face large and growing structural deficits largely due to known demographic trends. Our current fiscal policy is unsustainable."

David Walker, former Comptroller General of The United States

The demographic shifts in our country will impact all of us, personally. Not only will the cost of living continue to increase, but also the cost of our Federal Government. It is projected that an average 45-year-old couple will receive benefits from the government totaling $884,000, 45% more than they would receive today. The government has created a social dependency problem that has a need and addiction equal to that of a drug addict, living on the streets. The government's ability to pay for this addiction depends on us, the taxpayers.

"Addressing the nation's transformational challenges may take a generation or more to resolve. Given the size of the projected deficits, the U.S. Government will not be able to grow its way out of this problem – tough choices are required."

David Walker, former Comptroller General of The United States

Understanding the problem that we will all be facing certainly will give you a clearer view to look at decisions you have made in the past and the ones you need to make for the future. Understanding that, at this time in your life, this may be the lowest tax bracket you will ever be in, is important. The government, because of its own actions, is now conceding that taxes must go up in the future. Your ability to accept the idea that taxes will go up in your personal life is not a concession of total defeat, only a concession that it will be a problem, and we need to pay attention to it now.

The first two defining moments we have discussed so far – *Your money will never be worth more than it is today* and *This may be the lowest tax bracket you will ever be in* - are unique because they will have a direct impact on all the remaining lessons. They also present a very clear challenge to our thought process. Together, they question some of the traditional thinking that has been branded into all of us.

If your money will never be worth more than it is today, due to inflation, and this is the lowest tax bracket you will ever be in, due to demographics, then why is traditional thinking telling you to take as much of today's money as you can and throw it as far as you can into the future – where it will have less buying power and be taxed the most? Is that the type of thought process or planning you want to pursue?

When you apply these two lessons to your everyday lives, you may perceive things a little differently. If I purchase a car that is a depreciating asset anyway, do I want to use as many of today's dollars that have the most buying power and pay that car off as fast as I can? Do I want to buy that car with the most buying power dollars that I have or the least? I would like to drive the nicest car I could with the least amount of monthly payment. Remember, at 3% inflation, $1,000 has the buying power of $744 in ten years. Would you want to make more mortgage payments on your house with today's dollars or more payments ten years from now when the buying power of that payment is lower? As discussed earlier, banks and finance companies are well aware that the dollars they get from you and me will never be worth more to them than they are right now. Their marketing may even urge you to make additional loan payments. They know and understand the importance of today's dollars.

These two lessons may also lead you to think about the way you are approaching your retirement dollars. In qualified plans, such as IRAs, 401Ks, etc., you must understand that you are simply deferring the tax table to a later date when you take the money out. Whether you retire to a lower or higher tax bracket may depend on how much you were able to save for retirement. One thing is very clear though, because of demographic shifts and the spending of the Federal Government, taxes must go up. Thirty or forty percent of your retirement dollars could go to just paying taxes. Then you must consider: With what you have left after taxes, what will be the buying power of that money at that time? Understanding this may open your eyes to other ideas other than today's traditional thinking.

"Tax-rate increases of sufficient dimensions to deal with our looming fiscal problems arguably pose significant risks to economic growth. This dramatic demographic change is certain to place enormous demands on our nation's resources."

Alan Greenspan, Testimony to the U.S. House of Representatives

Defining Moment #3

You can't do the same things over and over and expect different results.

Einstein once said, "You cannot solve a problem using the same thought process that created the problem in the first place." This is true in our daily lives. Every day we face new challenges and new problems. The average person reading this book will face at least two crises or major problems each year. More times than not, we find ways of dealing with and controlling some of these problems. Many times, we do not solve these problems but simply manage them, so they blend into our daily lives. In some ways, this is how our government approaches its problems. The government spends most of its time and money (our money) and most of its energy managing problems. It will use some form of semi-solution and compromises to address the problem, instead of really solving the problem.

Stephen Covey contends that a paradigm is a way of thinking. It is a map or a plan, but no matter how hard we work, having the wrong map or plan will not get us to our destination regardless of our behavior, attitude, or diligence.

Our financial success is centered on a way of thinking. It is a map to the future with a planned or, in many cases, an uncertain destination. The difference between success and failure of reaching your financial goals will greatly depend on your way of thinking and your plan. Without knowledge, a process of thinking, and basic rules to follow, you most certainly will get lost.

We Are Creatures of Habit

I am assuming many of you went to school. How many of you ever crammed for a test the night before or worked to finish a report or project that was due the next day? You know you fooled around until the last minute, knowing you could stay up all night and study for the test, or still get the project done. This thought process that we learned in our early years became part of our lives. This process of how we approached school, work, and our everyday lives became socially acceptable. The thought process that was in place at that time of our lives came down to this: How do I get the best possible score or result with the least amount of time and effort? While this way of thinking is socially accepted, in many ways, it does not give the best results.

Imagine, for a moment, that you owned a farm. Can you imagine using the thought process of "cramming" on a farm? Imagine forgetting to plant the seeds for your crops in the spring. Then you decided to fool around most of the summer with the intent of planting seeds late in the summer, then cramming in the fall to bring home the harvest. During that time, can you imagine neglecting to milk the cows for a couple of weeks because you wanted some time off? Why is the lesson of "cramming" acceptable at school or work but not on the farm? You see, your success at school or work is based on socially accepted laws, while the farm's success is based on natural laws.

Your financial success will be based on a thought process and on natural laws – the laws of the farm. Financial success will take a lot of work and planning. It will take proper management, planting, and cultivating. But, most importantly, it will take a lot of time. You cannot continue to do the same things over and over again that you learned using social laws and expect different results where natural laws govern.

Twenty-Four – Seven

We need to pay attention to what is happening in our everyday lives. Financial institutions such as banks, credit card companies, investment and broker-age firms, mortgage companies, and the government have hired marketing companies, think tanks, and psychologists. The focus of these groups is how to separate people, you and me, from our money. These companies never rest. They are planning constantly, twenty-four hours a day, seven days a week, on how to achieve their goals. The question I have: How much time are we spending defending ourselves from these groups? Are we paying attention to how much money we are actually giving away or transferring away to these people? Many of us spend more time every year planning our vacations than we do planning our future.

Solving Someone Else's Problem

If we continue to approach and plan for our future using a traditional thought process, we may find ourselves in a vicious cycle. We are told in order to secure our financial future we must save more. The idea here is to hope that our money will compound itself into greater wealth. There are a few guarantees that come along with traditional thinking and traditional planning. First, you may be the only one taking the risk in trying to make your money grow. Second, the person who recommended this course of action will get paid, the companies you invested in will get paid, and the government will get paid via taxes. You will be the last person to get paid, if you get paid at all. Remember, all of this is happening with YOUR money. From a distance, it may seem you are solving a lot of other people's financial problems while attempting to solve your own.

Breaking the Cycle

You may find yourself caught up in the evolution of transferring away a great deal of your money to those who create the situation, control the outcomes, and profit from it. Let's face it: The banks, mortgage companies, credit card companies, investment firms, and the government deal with you in a fashion that they are guaranteed to get paid at some point in time. Although they will not admit it, they need you and your money to survive. It is a little funny how their marketing makes you feel that you need them. A credit card's advertisement shows a number of people paying for hamburgers with a credit card and how simple and easy life is until someone in line is dumb enough to use cash and messes up the whole flow of doing business. The social implication is that you will feel dumb for not using your credit card for that purchase or any other purchases. The goal of that credit card company may be that they hope that one of their credit card users will be late with their payment for that five-dollar hamburger so that they can assess a $25 or $30 late fee.

By breaking the cycle of transferring your wealth away to others, you get to keep more of your money. If someone is earning $75,000 in income per year, and they manage to save $5,000, they would have $70,000 of residual income left. This $70,000 is typically spent on mortgage payments, car payments, food, clothing, education, taxes, etc., and those payments sustain their standard of living. Like most average families, at the end of the year, the $70,000 has been spent and there is no extra money left. Look up 'extra money' in *Webster's Dictionary*; it doesn't exist. If this person could save just 1% of that $70,000 of residual income, it would create $700 in savings. That savings represents a 14% increase on the $5,000 that they *were* saving. That's right, a 14% rate of return with no market risk, guaranteed. They did not have to buy any product to do this. When people learn how to recapture transferred dollars, they will typically save more than 1% of their residual income. It is not uncommon that the average person can save as much as 5% to 7% of their residual income.

Still, traditional thinking is going about the business of trying to prove that the world is still flat. That nothing has changed and nothing needs to. Traditional thinking contends that your success in the future depends on nothing more than the right selection of slot machines of life where you are the only one at risk. The casinos of life attract a lot of people with one dream dangled in front of them; they just might win.

One might ask, "So why do we continue to do the same thing over and over again?" Well, when you look at it, we are really limited in the types of investments we can make. We can invest in stocks and mutual funds, qualified plans, real estate, and bank saving programs. Inside these types of programs, you can invest in a million different ways, but if asked, the typical person might respond by saying they have stocks, mutual funds, a 401K, etc. Simply owning something does not mean you know how it works. We merely identify them, and unfortunately, in most cases, financially this is all we know. Psychologically, the average person does not like to admit that they have made mistakes, and are reluctant to admit they do not know something. This is a problem. It shuts down any thought process that may be different. The big question though is this: How can you say yes or no to ideas that you don't even know exist? How can you be aware of something you're not aware of?

You see, your economic situation is a matter of choice, not a matter of chance. Many financial decisions are misguided and are made with a lack of knowledge. Driven by fear, yet cautious of change, many financial decisions are made by default, without knowledge, and unaware of any future unintended consequences. You have had to make difficult financial decisions in your life. These decisions were made with information and knowledge you had at that time. Today, if you received more information and more knowledge, you may want to review some of the decisions you made in the past. Change can be a good thing.

Recognizing that we cannot be aware of things we don't know about will be a transformation in your thought process. In your everyday life, you will have a different perspective of things around you. You may view the way you purchase your home or autos differently. The tax savings in your retirement plans may come into question. The way you approach retirement may change dramatically. You will discover that the rate of return on your money and where it is may not be as important as how to use your money. Learning how money works will be the most important lesson of the day. Different results in your life will never occur if you continue to do the same things over and over again. We must pay attention to what is going on around us.

Defining Moment #4

Learn what is true and
what is not true.

If something you thought to be true was not true, when would you want to know about it? In today's world with all the information from the media, radio, TV, and websites, the truth can be redefined and actually be transformed into something that is not true. One lesson has become: If we repeat something over and over again, it will become ingrained in our minds that it must be true. Marketing companies use these tactics when marketing their products. So does the financial-services industry. Politicians have mastered the art of double talk, misstatements, misinformation, and repeated lies. They are under the delusion that we believe them and the mistaken impression that we need them. The media feeds us a relentless amount of garbage. It has become nothing more than "wannabe" actors giving their opinions, and trying to shape society to their image. All of this of course is my opinion, not fact. In opinion, you can agree with me or not. Either way, it is okay.

A myth is sort of funny. It is an idea that can be proven somewhat true on one hand and proven false on another. Typically, myths will occur when the results are not predictable by fact. Fact can become myth as new things are discovered and learned. Mankind knows a lot about what it knows, and very little about the rest. Heck, it took us a long time to get over the idea that the earth was not flat. I am afraid that we are going to have to get over a lot of other things we think is true, but again, that is just my opinion. When it comes to myth, one's opinion may become more compelling than actual facts involved. Someone declaring that a newborn baby is ugly will never convince the mother of that baby that her child is ugly, even though in a cute sort of way, it is. Myth is something that can be argued with a combination of fact and opinion. Whether it is true or not is in the eye of the beholder.

What if you realized you could make a lot of money selling a product that would not do exactly what it was advertised to do, but your advertising was so compelling that people bought it anyway? Selling this product made you rich. Would you ever feel compelled to tell, as they say, the rest of the story about how the product you sold them might not work? The truth is: probably not. The reality is we probably buy a lot of things with a little bit of myth attached to it.

A fact is a fact. It is what it is. Someone saying it is cold outside (opinion) is different from someone saying it is 20 degrees Fahrenheit outside (fact). An Eskimo may not think 20 degrees is very cold when the person from Florida might be shivering. I know, from the medical knowledge that we now possess, that I am going to die someday. Now I don't mind dying, but I just don't want to be there when it happens. But, I will die. That is a fact. Now here is a new phrase. It may be "logical and reasonable" to assume, since it is a fact that I am going to die, that I also might live a long time based on information that is medically known about me. One could argue that I could die by accident at any moment. So, my living a long time could be somewhat of a myth (myth). Does all of this sound confusing? Yes, because it is. We get all of our information on different levels of myth, opinion, fact, and truth. It is not impossible to get various amounts of all four when discussing anything. We get all our information from different groups who represent different things and have different agendas. More knowledge and more education will help you cut through the difference between myth and reality, fact and fiction.

Learning what is true and what is not true can be complicated. The difference between what is happening and what is not happening can also be alarming. As an example, let's say someone invested $1,000 over time and received an average 20% return for two years. How much would that person have at the end of two years?

A. $1,440
B. $1,280
C. $ 800
D. $ 0.00

Many people with calculators will answer that the person would have $1,440. That is correct. A 20% rate of return compounded annually for two years is $1,440. So, what this person heard from his planner or read in a prospectus, newspaper, or magazine article about the 20% average rate of return may cause someone to assume that they have accumulated

$1,440. That was pretty simple, right? But let's take a look at answer B, $1,280. If someone invested $1,000, and in the first year, they received a 60% rate of return and in the second year they lost 20%, they would have still averaged 20% for two years, but in the end they would only have $1,280. So, answer A and B are both right. Now, I am starting to think, if A and B are correct, I better look at answer C too. If someone invested $1,000 and in the first year received a 100% rate of return but lost 60% in the second year, they still averaged 20% a year, but the result is dramatically different. They would only have $800. Wow, how can a simple question have so many answers? Now I hate to do this, but let's look at answer D, $0.00. If the investment of $1,000 received a 140% rate of return in the first year and then lost 100% the second year (one hundred percent loss means you lost everything), you would still have an average of 20% for two years but have no money left. Holy cow, understanding what is true and what is not true, all of a sudden, got really complicated. No wonder people are confused. It wouldn't surprise me if some companies try to confuse you on purpose. Their marketing proudly advertises that their investors have received an average 20% rate of return over the last two years. Sounds good, right? Everyone must learn to pay attention to what is going on. It is critical.

Average vs. Actual

In trying to decipher what is true and what is not true, common sense and reality can take a back seat to marketing hype. Sometimes things that are happening in your everyday life can be confusing, such as rates of return. Look at the average rates of return compared to the actual rates of return in the Dow Jones Industrial Average. If you look at the average rates of return in the Dow from the beginning of the year 2000 to the end of 2006, the Dow average rate of return for each year looks like this:

The Dow Jones Industrial

2000	-6.17%
2001	-7.10%
2002	-16.76%
2003	25.32%
2004	3.15%
2005	- 0.61%
2006	16.29%

For these seven years, the average of the averages of the Dow was 2.02%. If you had invested $100,000 at the beginning of 2000 and received an average rate of return of 2.02%, by the end of 2006, you would have accumulated $115,003.77. Here is the funny part. If you actually had invested $100,000 in 2000 and kept your money in the Dow until the end of 2006, the amount of money you actually accumulated was $108,408.71. That calculated to a 1.16% return on your money. The difference between the average of the Dow and what you actually earned in the Dow was $6,595.06. That difference represents a 57% disparity between the average (2.02%) and the actual (1.16%) returns.

Understanding the math calculations is simple. If you have a 2.02% average for seven years, every year there is a positive number to calculate. The reality is that there were some negative-return years during that seven-year period.

If grandpop would have invested $100,000 in 1929, the average for the Dow from 1929 through 2006 is 6.81%. At 6.81%, that $100,000 would have grown to $17,023,080. If he actually had the money in the Dow all those years, what he actually accumulated was $4,154,089.42. That is a 71% difference between the average and the actual. Once again, the perception of what we believe to be true and what is really true could surprise you. What you have to learn and understand is that the statement that the Dow average of 2.02% from 2000 through 2006 is TRUE, but it does not represent actual results.

You'll Probably What?

As I discussed before, one of the most common financial phrases that has been driven into our heads over the last fifty years is: You will probably retire to two-thirds of your income, thus be in a lower tax bracket. If this is the wisdom of traditional thinking for lowering your taxes at retirement, one could come to the conclusion that with the same thought process someone could say – "I'm not saving for retirement, so I won't have to pay any taxes." This is what I call "the problem controlling the outcome" type of solution. With the idea of reducing someone's income to reduce taxes is a simple goal to achieve for some amateur planners. Too much time is being spent on the thought process of planning for controlled failure.

By ignoring the changes that we will be facing in the future, the declining benefits, the increasing taxation, aging population, and a smaller tax-paying work force, retiring to two-thirds of your income is not a choice, it is a mistake.

Your Dollar and the Future

Any conversation you may have about your future financial life would be incomplete without taking into consideration how inflation will impact your money. Without understanding the buying power of your future dollars, your planning may come up considerably short of the money you will need to support your lifestyle at retirement. When you retire, you will continue to spend money but discover that it seems everything costs just a little bit more than it used to cost. The problem is, costs continue to rise while you are on a fixed income. No one should be surprised that increases in the cost of living happen; it has been going on forever. The surprise is that while you were planning for retirement, the inflation factor was not planned for or even discussed.

Defining Moment number one, "Your money will never be worth more than it is today" is a lesson that you fully need to understand if you want to learn how money works. Many people retire and sit around discussing "the good old days." Well, in my good old days, gas was twenty cents a gallon; stamps were three cents; you could get two loaves of bread for a quarter, and my first house cost $18,000. Oh, the good old days were great, but then you remember that your income back then was only one tenth of what it is today.

If you look at one thousand dollars today, it represents the maximum buying power that these dollars will ever have. When you apply a three percent inflation factor to money, you will discover that in ten years the buying power of $1,000 is now only $744. It also means that to have the same buying power of $1,000 in ten years, you will need $1,343.

Incomes in the United States, when adjusted for inflation, have not increased your buying power over the last 20 years. During that 20-year period though, personal taxes have increased 42% faster than personal incomes. State and local government taxes have increased about 168% faster than national incomes in that same period of time. In 1928, a worker needed to work 1.4 months to pay for federal, state, and local government spending. Today, a worker needs to work 5.1 months to pay their taxes.

Over the past several years, inflation has driven up costs substantially. The costs of health insurance, education, heat and energy, property insurance, gas, goods, clothing, property taxes, purchasing cars, and even the cost of having some fun have gone up faster than our incomes. These costs will continue to rise for the rest of our lives. You'd better start planning for it now.

One last issue that impacts the buying power of your money is the actual value of the American dollar when compared to other currencies. The U.S. dollar used to be able to buy goods cheaper because our currency was of higher value than the currency of the country where the goods were made. Recently, the value of the U.S. dollar has slipped considerably. This should be a concern to everyone. Your financial future depends on the buying power of the dollar.

Your House – Donald Trump and the Bank

In learning to decipher what is true and what is not, let's examine the way someone pays for their home. There can be a lot of conversations about the type of mortgage you should have or whether you should pay cash or pay off your home as fast as you can. All of this can be very confusing.

First of all, almost everyone will agree that a bank or mortgage company stands to make a lot of money from interest payments in a mortgage. Why then do they try to entice you into making additional payments on your home; so that you will save interest? It sounds like really bad marketing on the part of the bank or mortgage company. Well, the real answer is that the lending institutions understand Defining Moment #1: Money will never be worth more than it is today. Second, they understand the velocity of money. If a bank spends a dollar five and a half times, wouldn't you think that they want to get their hands on as many dollars as they can NOW? Talking you into making additional payments will help them far more than it will help you.

If Donald Trump wanted to buy a building for one million dollars, would he simply write a check for a million dollars and buy it? No. He would meet with his advisors and pay the least amount he could to secure the property, drive the value up, and then sell it. He wants to use the least amount of today's dollars to gain control of the property. He does not pay cash for the property because he would be giving up today's dollars to do it, and he knows that by paying cash, or the highest payment he could, does not increase the value of the property. So why is the advice you receive from the banks or mortgage company about paying your house off as fast as you can (the most payment) different from what Mr. Trump would do? Would you rather receive financial information from Donald Trump or the bank? The only difference between Donald Trump and the banks is that only one of them makes money from you.

The Largest Investment
of Your Life

You have been told by almost everyone that your home is the largest and greatest investment that you will ever make. To many, owning a home is the most misunderstood American dream. There is a lot of information that concludes that rising housing prices made buying a home one of the greatest investments you could ever make. There are many factors that can impact the value of a house. Mortgage interest rates, property taxes, property insurance, changing neighborhoods, and the general economy can wreak havoc with home values. In order to qualify for purchasing a home, someone must prove they have the income and ability to make not only the mortgage payment, but also to pay the taxes and insurance. Almost everyone would agree that insurance rates and property taxes will continue to go up. The problem is there may come a time where you may have to reduce the price of your home to sell it because the taxes, interest rates, and insurance eat up more of the monthly money a new buyer qualified for. If a new buyer qualified for an $850 monthly payment, with a 5.5% 30-year mortgage, the new buyer could purchase a $150,000 home. But, if interest rates went up to 8%, that new buyer would only qualify for a $116,000 home with an $851 monthly mortgage payment. In order to sell your home to that buyer, you would have to lower the price of your home from $150,000 to $116,000. That is a $34,000 loss in value to you.

Let's take a look at the house as an investment. Nine years ago, you purchased a home for $175,000, and nine years later, the value of that house is $250,000. That seems like a pretty good investment, right? That increase of $75,000 over a nine-year period calculates to a 4.04% rate of return on the value of that house. Improvements you made on the house during the nine years you lived there totaled $20,000. You know, stuff like a new roof, remodeling the kitchen, and redoing a bathroom add up. With the $20,000 of improvements added in, the rate of return on your house is now 2.8%. If you look at your house as an investment, you may be interested in the after-tax rate of return on the growth in value in your house. If you paid $3,000 in property taxes each year, the after-tax rate of return on the increase value of your house is 1.33%. Believe it or not. That is a little different than "the greatest investment in your life."

Learning what is true and what is not true will change your life dramatically. Having choices in life decisions will help you recapture money that you may be giving away unknowingly and unnecessarily.

The Exact Day

Wouldn't you like to know the exact day that your 401K or IRA plan will suffer its greatest loss? If you knew that day and could do something today to eliminate or reduce that loss, would you do it? Most likely, the day your 401K or IRA will suffer its greatest loss is the day you retire and start taking income from these plans. The taxes you will have to pay to get your money out of these plans could be 20%, 30%, or 40% and may be even higher. It may be possible that when you take your money out of these programs you could be in a higher tax bracket than when you put the money in the program. The only way you can win in a qualified program is if you retire to the SAME or LOWER tax bracket. Now remember Defining Moment #2: Today, you are probably in the lowest tax bracket you will ever be in for the rest of your life.

A Later Date

Hearing the words "tax deferred" almost creates some idea that a magical moment in your life is about to take place. Qualified plans do not eliminate taxes; they simply defer the tax table to a later date. Do you believe taxes will be lower in the future? Of course not. Government spending and the changing demographics in our country almost guarantee tax increases in the future. Knowing this creates an interesting question: When do you want to take money out of qualified plans? When taxes are the lowest or when they are the highest? Understanding what is myth and what is reality and what is true or not true will change the way you think.

True or Not True

If you take money out of an IRA before the age of 59½, what happens? Well, you have crossed over into "no-no" land. It is a good possibility that you will be labeled as crazy and you will have to lay low for a few weeks until that cloud of stupidity hanging over you disappears. For taking the money out of an IRA prematurely, you will be "taxed and penalized" – now go to your room; you're grounded.

Let's take a step back, take a deep breath, and look at the phrase "taxed and penalized." First of all, whether you take money out of an IRA before or after the age of 59½, you will be taxed on the money you take out. NO SURPRISE HERE, so you can come out of hiding for a little while. Some professionals confuse the issue of delaying a tax with not having to pay a tax at all. That is just silly. Perhaps they believe taxes will be lower in the future.

Now, let's look at the "penalized" portion of your sin of withdrawing money out of an IRA before the age of 59½. It is possible to withdraw money from an IRA before the age of 59½ WITHOUT incurring an IRS penalty. IRS notice 89-25-IRB 1989-12.68 section 72t allows premature distributions of IRA funds by using one of the three following distribution methods:

1. Life Expectancy
2. Amortization
3. Annuitization

The life expectancy method simply calculates the amount that can be withdrawn annually, by dividing your account balance by your life expectancy based on the tables furnished by the IRS. The second method is amortization, which allows you to amortize your account balance based on a projection of what your account might earn over your lifetime. The IRS requires that the interest rate assumed in this calculation be "reasonable." For the annuitization method, the IRS also allows withdrawal based on a life insurance mortality table and a reasonable interest rate assumption. This method usually generates the largest withdrawal without penalty.

Really True

Remember, qualified plans offer a couple of guarantees in most cases. 401Ks and IRAs are guaranteed to be taxed, and you are the only one at risk in your quest to get higher rates of return. If you can block out these two realities, then I guess these plans are okay.

Is That a Monkey on Your Back

In discussing what is true and what we think is true in our financial future, we need to discuss the government. There is no other group of people who will impact your financial future more than the government will. Good or bad, you and I, the taxpayers, will be paying the price and carrying the load for everything they do. You see, the government is not a business that earns money to pay for all their programs. Their real job is to collect money from you and me in the form of taxes to pay for everything they do. They spend all this money with virtually no risk to them.

In this conversation about the government, the goal is not to determine fault, who said what, or who is lying. I would rather discuss the position that the government has put us in when it comes to our personal financial futures. The government is playing fast and loose when it comes to the truth and money. The financial burden they have created for us to carry will go beyond our generation and into the next two or three generations of Americans. To justify their economic spending, the government must calculate the tax revenues they will receive from the un-dead but also the future tax revenues from the unborn.

The truth is, government spending is out of control. It continues to spend about 30% more than it takes in. The truth is, according to David Walker, the former Comptroller General of the United States, balancing the budget by the year 2040 could require cutting federal spending by 60% or raising federal taxes to nearly two times today's level. The truth is, closing the long-term fiscal gap of the government would require real average annual economic growth in the double-digit range every year for the next 75 years. The U.S. economy grew an average 3.2% in the boom years of the 1990s. The truth is that government decisions have strapped us with a mountain of debt that has enslaved us as a nation, and it seems as if no one is paying attention and no one cares.

I want to encourage you to visit the GAO's website and "Debt To The Penny," a U.S. treasury website, for a reality check.

In conclusion, the government's own audit report states this: "More troubling still, the federal government's financial condition and long-term fiscal outlook is continuing to deteriorate...Addressing the nation's transformational challenge may take a generation or more to resolve. Given the size of the projected deficit, the U.S. Government will not be able to grow its way out of this problem. Tough choices are required."

That's Not a Monkey on Your Back –
That's a Gorilla

Can the average American borrow their way to prosperity? The answer is no. Years ago, America was based on strong family values. We were a "pay as you go" nation that learned the value of incomes and savings. Today, America has become a nation of consumers that has attached liens and promissory notes on much of its future income. Debt ratios of the average American household have reached record highs. This is far different than the founding fathers of our nation could ever imagine. In the future, there will be unintended consequences in paying for the debts we carry.

Household debt ratios in the United States have increased almost 90% faster than the growth of the economy since the late 1960s when real median family incomes stopped rising. This suggests that real equity and savings have not been the driving force for economic growth. The growth of the economy is driven by debt.

More American families' futures are now at the mercy of available credit and interest rates. Many households are more dependent on debt than the incomes they earn and the cash flow they have. In the past 30 years, inflation-adjusted incomes for males in the United States have dropped about nine percent. Personal savings during that same time frame have plummeted 114% to its lowest level since 1934, during the Great Depression. All the while Americans have been on a spending binge well beyond the growth of their incomes. Economist Ludwig Van Meses stated that the end results brought on by reckless expansion of credit (debt)... "There is no means of avoiding the final collapse of a boom brought about by credit (debt) expansion. The alternative is only whether the crisis should come sooner as a result of a voluntary abandonment of further credit (dept) expansion, or later as a final and total catastrophe of the currency system involved."

> *"No generation has a right to contract debts greater than can be paid off during the course of its own existence."*
>
> George Washington

Controlling and reducing debt is very important. Some in Washington would have you believe that increasing prices dramatically will help control and reduce our use on energy. That increasing the taxes on energy will make us conserve more energy. If that is the case, then solving personal debt in the country will be easy. Simply raise the price of everything, so no one can afford to buy anything and give credit to only a very few. Makes sense, huh!?

What is true is that spending, whether excessive spending by the government or excessive personal spending, is something that we will have to deal with...sooner or later.

The process of learning the defining moments, and discovering what is true and what is not true in your everyday life, can create dramatic changes in your financial future. Understanding how your money works for you, not others, is the center point in changing the way you think. From now on, the way you think will impact your future. It is now time to think about the money in your life from a different perspective.

Defining Moment #5

The Three Types of Money

One of the most powerful discoveries you can make is that understanding how money works will change your life. What is more important than where your money is, and its rate of return, is knowing how it works. You may think that learning how money works would be a massive undertaking on your part, but it does not have to be that difficult. You must first learn how to categorize your money. This will simplify your thought process and enable you to improve your life. You have been marketed to death by companies telling you that all you have to do is to have the right products and higher rates of return to make your life better. Now, while that is important, the main focus of this marketing is for you to buy something. It sounds easy, and there is very little thinking involved. That type of marketing is aimed at the person whose life is so busy that he has very little time to pay attention. Remember, the product they sell is not the source for your knowledge; it should be the result of your knowledge. Owning more products does not make you smarter. With that being said, both you and I are going to need some products in the future. The point is that the products we have are not the center point of our knowledge. They are tools we use. Products alone will not teach you how money works.

> *The products you purchase are not the source of your knowledge; they should be the result of your knowledge.*

Your thought process should begin with understanding the types of money you have. If you categorize your money into three types, then controlling your money will become easier. The three types of money will help you identify mistakes, problems, and solutions that surround your everyday life.

Power

The greatest financial tool you possess is your ability to earn money and generate an income stream. This continuous flow of new money is the heart of your financial life. This income can come from various sources. You can receive compensation from your career or occupation. Unless you work until you die, this source of money may end at retirement or, heaven forbid, you lose your job, or even worse yet, you become disabled, unable to work again for the rest of your life. For many, working until you die is not an option – it is a necessity. For others, an income flow can come from retirement plans and/or investments. This source of income is secured as the result of some planning in the past. Another source of income flow can come from government programs and benefits. These benefits, and the income stream they produce, are becoming less and less certain to be there in the future. The demographic shifts, a decreasing work force, and an aging population are ingredients that may reduce or eliminate these benefits in the future. No matter what the source of your income is, it remains one of your most valuable assets. It is important to remember Defining Moment Number One: Your money will never be worth more than it is today. Let's now divide your money into three specific groups.

Show Me the Money

Your money is going to end up in one of three categories: lifestyle money, accumulated money, and money you transfer away, sometimes unknowingly and unnecessarily. Every dollar you have will filter through one or more of these categories. Your thought process can be simplified by being able to identify how money passes through your life. Being able to track how your money enters and exits your life will uncover lessons you need to learn in understanding how money works.

Lifestyle Money

Your standard of living, the way you live, has taken a lifetime to achieve. Maintaining and increasing your lifestyle for the remainder of your life should be everyone's goal. Your lifestyle money is the amount of money you need to maintain your current standard of living. The house you live in, the cars you drive, your vacations, the country clubs, all the comforts you are accustomed to – they all fall into the category of lifestyle money. You have worked very hard, and you deserve an affordable quality of life. You are certainly aware of your lifestyle money more than the other types of money because you live and spend money on your lifestyle almost every day. Many of the financial decisions that you make are centered on your standard of living. Unfortunately, the cost of your standard of living continues to increase every year due to inflation.

> *The financial knowledge you have today will determine your lifestyle in the future.*

If you attempt to live above the standard of living that you can afford, you can run the risk of being buried in personal debt.

The challenge of maintaining your standard of living after your working years can get complicated. You may find yourself on somewhat of a fixed income at retirement. If you followed traditional thinking and achieved the goal of retiring on two-thirds of your working income, your lifestyle could suffer dramatic changes. You may discover that everything you buy will continue to increase in price along with the taxes you pay on these goods. At 3% inflation, a dollar when you are 65 will have the buying power of fifty-five cents 20 years later.

The majority of money you earn will end up in your lifestyle. It will consume an increasing amount of money in the future. A problem occurs when people start to fund their lifestyle with an increasing amount of debt and credit.

Accumulated Money

Accumulated money is that portion of your earnings that you attempt to save. With our best attempts and intentions, some of our money ends up in investments, saving programs, retirement plans, and banks. The average American is finding it more and more difficult to save and accumulate money. According to the GAO, the Government Accountability Office, we are saving at the lowest rate, per capita, since 1934 during the Great Depression. There are many reasons why this is happening, but the result of this is a great concern. Our inability to fund our future lifestyles will impact everyone.

Banks, financial planners, and investment brokers are all competing for the money you are attempting to save. In the financial world, there is an enormous amount of information. You would think with all the financial magazines, news articles, TV and radio shows, and a record number of financial experts out there that it would be almost impossible to lose money. It has turned out to be quite the opposite. All of this information has caused a lot of confusion. Misinformation and the "sleight of hand" make good financial sound bites and headlines. For the average American trying to save, it is becoming more difficult to separate opinions from fact, myth from reality, and the truth from fiction. Greed and ambition motivate individuals, and

> *How much time do you want to spend on reducing your lifestyle to save more money?*

corporations forgo the truth whenever it is convenient and profitable.

You may discover that your accumulated money may be the smallest category or type of money that you have, but the most important. Your future and financial survival depend upon it. Your ability to save more money and increase your lifestyle will depend on understanding and controlling the third type of money in your life.

Transferred Money

The third and last category of money in your life is transferred money. It may surprise you that many people transfer away much of their wealth on an everyday basis, unknowingly and many times unnecessarily. Transfers of your wealth appear in the form of taxes, interest rates, finance fees, finance charges, maintenance and management fees, etc. The beneficiaries of these transfers are the federal, state, and local governments; banks; loan companies; and mortgage and investment companies. While everyone is focusing on their lifestyle and accumulated money, the answers to increasing your wealth lay hidden in the transfers of your wealth. Learning to recognize, understand, and recapture the transfers in your life will allow you to create more wealth without spending one more dime than you are already spending or facing any additional market risks. The more transfers of your wealth that you are involved in, the more your lifestyle and accumulated money decrease.

You should learn to categorize all of your money. Your money ends up supporting your lifestyle, being saved and invested for your future, or being transferred away. Unfortunately, any attempt to increase your income, improve your standard of living, and save money for your future also triggers some unintended consequences in your life. As you increase your lifestyle and your savings, you will incur an increase in taxes now and possibly in the future. Even increasing the amount you save for retirement today could create greater amounts of taxation in the future. It seems every time you try to save a dollar, you will have to give a dollar away.

> *You unknowingly and unnecessarily transfer away much of your wealth.*

While expanding your standard of living, you purchase new homes, cars, televisions, home improvements, furniture, and many other items. Sometimes these goods are bought on credit. This debt has interest rates attached to it, which transfers some of your money to others. Let's face it: Almost all the purchases in your lifestyle are depreciating assets and get replaced from time to time. When you buy a new car, by the time you drive it out of the dealership, the car value drops about 30% and continues to drop in value every year. Even purchasing a home is surrounded by transfers in the form of interest rates, property taxes, school taxes, water and sewer taxes, maintenance and improvement costs, and insurance costs.

Many banks and mortgage and credit companies look at your buying habits as "a dollar from you is a dollar for me" opportunity. Unfortunately, with the possible exception of the mortgage interest you pay, almost all your other debt interest is not tax deductible. As you can see, these transfers can consume a lot of your money.

If you have the opportunity to recapture many of the dollars you are transferring to others and keep the money for yourself, would you do it? Absolutely! Unfortunately, most people do not know how to do this. There is a reason why no one is teaching you how to recapture transfers. If the banks, credit card companies, mortgage companies, investment companies, and the government taught you how to reduce your payments to them, well, they would get less of your money. These companies understand the lesson of the first defining moment we discussed. They know that money will never be worth more than it is today. Their goal is simple: to get as much of "your money" today, where it will have the most buying power for them. Many Americans find themselves in the position of having to work so hard to pay for all these transfers in their lives that they do not have time to learn how to reduce or eliminate them.

Follow That Dollar

Let's take a look at how the three types of money can impact your life. Just in time for your favorite sport season, you have decided to buy your wife a new 60-inch, plasma, flat-screen television. You have figured that you earned enough income the last couple of weeks to purchase the gift. But, before you receive your pay from the income you earned, the company deducts federal taxes, state taxes, city taxes, social security tax, and Medicare taxes. Envision, if you can, your dollars passing through the transfer part of your money before it got to your lifestyle portion of your life. The money you now have is considerably less than what you earned after the transfer of taxes occurred. After passing through the taxes, your money is now in your lifestyle. Now you are ready to buy "the gift." You go to the electronic store, and after about 20 minutes of intense comparison shopping, you find "the gift" you want. I mean the one your wife will love. Now you are faced with another dilemma: Do you pay cash or finance the gift? If you pay cash, not only do you lose the money you paid for the television, but also the ability to earn any money from that money once you spend it. This is called a lost opportunity cost. If you finance "the gift," you have to pay interest for the use of someone else's money (SEM). Financing the television will result in you paying more for "the gift" over time. Either way you purchase "the gift" will result in another transfer of wealth in your life. First, the money you could have earned from keeping your money and financing the gift, or second, paying interest on the loan for financing it. Regardless of how you pay for the television, you also have to pay a sales tax on top of the purchase price, which is another transfer.

So, for just trying to buy your wife a nice gift, your money had to go through federal, state, and city payroll taxes, social security taxes, Medicare taxes, and a sales tax. Plus, you either suffered a lost opportunity cost or you are paying interest to some finance or credit card company. Now that is a lot of transfers. The things some men have to go through just to try to make their wives happy.

Follow This Dollar

You are 45 years old. You have a nice career, and you are married to a nice man who showers you with gifts, most recently a 60-inch plasma television. This is just the latest of a long list of gifts that include power tools, fishing equipment, bowling balls, and a couple of dogs. You are truly a lucky woman. You realize that, although all of these things are nice, you are married to a spender.

Your financial makeup is a little different, and you save as much as you can. Where you work, your employer provides a 401K retirement plan for its workers. You take advantage of this benefit and deposit as much as you can into it. You have been told that by saving in the 401K that portion does not get taxed now. It defers the tax until you retire.

Try to envision how this dollar moves. A portion of the income you earn flows directly into your accumulated money without any transfers reducing that amount. Sounds good, but in order to get these dollars from the accumulated portion of your money to your lifestyle money, certain things must happen. First, you have to retire. Then, your accumulated money must flow through transferred money where it gets taxed and only then can it flow into your lifestyle money for you, I mean your husband, to spend. All the purchases you make from your lifestyle money will have more taxes, sales taxes, attached to them. You may have discovered the hard way that deferring taxes to a later date resulted in you paying more taxes in the future.

These are examples of how your money flows from one type of money to another in your life. Understanding how the money flows is the first step in learning to control your money and recognize the transfers. By learning this, you can reduce or eliminate these transfers in your life and you get to keep the money. Many of the types of transfers are buried in our everyday monetary transactions.

Defining Transfer Labels

It is one thing to be held up by someone wearing a mask and carrying a gun; it is another to willingly give away your money freely, but the result of either one in your personal financial life is the same. Just as you can identify a thief by his mask and gun, you must learn to identify the transfers in your life that also take money from you. Many people have not been trained to recognize these transfers. Quite the opposite, people have been trained and brainwashed to accept that these transfers are just a part of life. Some transfers in your life are inescapable, but many people create transfers in their life by the decisions they make or do not make. Bad judgment, bad investments, bad timing, indecisiveness, and sometimes doing nothing – all these can also create transfers and a loss of wealth to you. You must remember your economic situation is a matter of choice, not a matter of chance. The problem is that many of life's decisions are made by default, without enough knowledge, and these decisions can create unintentional consequences in your future. A transfer of your money is nothing more than profit for someone else. Now pay attention. The government sees you as a taxpayer. The bank sees you as a borrower and interest payer. Investment companies see you as a fee payer, nothing more, nothing less. These groups are not going to do you any favors. They are not your friends, and in most cases in dealing with them, you are the only one at risk. Here are transfers labels, what they are called, that are active in your everyday life.

Defining Transfers

TAXES: Taxes occur dozens of times a day in your daily life. There are federal, state, and local income taxes; sales taxes; telephone taxes; cell phone taxes; water and sewer taxes; gas taxes; business taxes; cable TV taxes; capital gains taxes; service taxes, and utility taxes. The list of taxes you pay goes on and on. Some of these taxes are unavoidable and impact everyone, whether you are still working or retired. Taxes impact your lifestyle, accumulated, and transferred money.

INTEREST RATES: Debt in America is at an all-time high. The interest on this debt is a great concern. The interest rate on much of this debt is flexible, meaning it can go up. Interest is paid on mortgages, equity lines of credit, credit cards, auto loans and leases, college loans, and various other purchases. Interest rate payments come from your lifestyle money, after taxes. Paying too much money on interest could impact your ability to deposit more money into savings and accumulated money.

BANK FEES: In my book *Learning To Avoid Unintended Consequences*, I list about 100 fees that a bank can charge you. Once again, bank fees are transfers that come from your lifestyle money: check fees, check-cashing fees, ATM fees, saving account fees, late fees, early withdrawal fees, etc. Why not just put on a mask, get a gun, and rob us while we are standing in line waiting for all that free service they proclaim to give us.

MAINTENANCE FEES: You gave them your money, then they want to charge you a fee for giving it to them. These fees once again are typically paid out of your lifestyle money. Many times, a maintenance fee is simply subtracted from the money you gave them. It is not enough that they use your money to make tons of money for themselves; they charge you a fee. Using your money must be some kind of nuisance to them.

MANAGEMENT FEES: Once again, these types of transfers are hidden from you by simply subtracting them from your accounts. Management fees guarantee the company of getting paid first, whether you gain money in their accounts or they lose it all for you.

Management fees are a transfer to your lifestyle and accumulated types of money.

FINANCE CHARGES: It is not enough that companies that lend you money charge you interest on the loans, they want to charge you finance charges for processing the paperwork, billing you and sending you a late payment notice, a late fee. These transfers, once again, impact your lifestyle money.

L.O.C.: If you pay a fee, a charge, an interest rate, or finance charge to some company, not only do you lose the dollar you gave them, but also the ability to earn money from the money you just gave to them. This compounds your financial troubles.

Product Transfers

Almost everything we attempt to do to help our financial situation results in some form of transfer. Following the financial advice of some experts, many times they gloss over or omit some of the transfers that you will have to face when purchasing financial products. I am not telling you not to buy financial products but rather to be aware of not only the positive aspects of your investment but also some of the transfers in your life that can and will occur from them. First of all, find competent professional help from someone who is versed in all aspects of products AND transfers.

Some of the most common places to invest your money are listed below, along with the possible transfers they possess:

CD and Bank Savings Accounts: Banks and credit unions offer a variety of ways to save money. These typically are savings accounts and certificates of deposit. Some savings accounts will have fees attached to them if your account falls below a minimum amount. Another transfer from these savings accounts is that you have to pay taxes on any gains or growth in these accounts. The Certificate of Deposit (CD) is usually associated with holding your money for a period of time, like six-month, one-year, three-year, and five-year CDs. If you withdraw money prematurely from these accounts, the bank will penalize you. You also have to pay tax on any gains you have in these accounts. These bank accounts typically have lower rates of return attached to them. TRANSFERS INVOLVED: FEES, EARLY WITHDRAWAL FEES, TAXES.

Mutual Funds: Putting money into mutual funds is common these days. They offer a variety of investment choices from aggressive to conservative, and each fund is diversified with a number of different companies or investments within itself. In many mutual funds, there are managers to run the fund, so they get paid. There also may be a front-end charge that you pay to buy the fund. There also may be an early-surrender fee. Inside the fund, there could be maintenance fees, and you will pay taxes on any gains that may come your way from the fund. Add to this that it is possible that you could lose money if the market goes down. TRANSFERS INVOLVED: MANAGEMENT FEES, POSSIBLE MAINTENANCE FEES, POSSIBLE FRONT-END LOAD FEES, POSSIBLE BACK-END FEES, TAXES, AND THE RISK OF LOSS FROM THE MARKET.

Real Estate: Real estate covers a wide range of investment possibilities. From buying your own home, rental property, commercial property, purchasing land, or the now popular "flipping" of property, you better know what you are doing in this game. When it comes to property, you can be smothered in transfers. Mortgage fees, closing costs, mortgage interest, down payment costs, insurances, property taxes, and many more costs can financially suffocate you. There is also the possibility that the value of the property could go down in value. Where you live and the property you buy can consume a large portion of your wealth. TRANSFERS INVOLVED: MORTGAGE FEES, PROPERTY TAXES, INSURANCE PREMIUMS, CLOSING COSTS, DOWN PAYMENTS, MORTGAGE INTEREST RATES, RISK OF VALUE GOING DOWN.

Stocks: Like mutual funds, purchasing stocks has become second nature to many people. I believe it is important to save and invest your money. Financial gains are needed for your future security. You know there is an element of risk when purchasing stocks. The companies marketing the stocks make it sound simple and everyone can play. You may quickly discover there is a price to pay to play. TRANSFERS INVOLVED: BROKERAGE FEES, MAINTENANCE FEES, TRADE FEES, MANAGEMENT FEES AND THE DREADED TAXES ON GAINS, AND THE POSSIBILITY OF LOSING MONEY, DUE TO DOWN MARKETS.

Annuities: For some time, mostly for the older generation, annuities offered some form of safety. There are fixed, variable, and index annuities. They offer a variety of results, some good, some not so good. The values inside an annuity grow tax-deferred, but at some point, the gains will be taxed either when you use the money or when you die. Annuities can carry some baggage. Exit fees can last very long and be very expensive. TRANSFERS INVOLVED: POSSIBLE LARGE EARLY WITHDRAWAL FEES, SURRENDER CHARGES, TAXES ON ANY GAINS WHEN YOU WITHDRAW MONEY OR ON ANY GAINS WHEN YOU DIE.

These are the types of products that you may have in your life right now or possibly in the near future. In no way am I saying you should not own any of these products. I believe you need as many financial tools as you can get. Learning how these tools work and how and when to use them is more important than owning a tool. Example, what good is a wrench to a dressmaker?

Review

To summarize this chapter, let's review the thought process we have established.

There are only three types of money in your life:

> Lifestyle Money
> Accumulated Money
> Transferred Money

Transfers are recognized as the following:

> Taxes
> Interest Rates
> Finance Charges
> Management Fees
> Bank Fees
> Maintenance Fees
> Lost Opportunity Costs

Many of the products we buy have transfers we discussed attached to them:

> Bank Savings Accounts
> CDs
> Mutual Funds
> Real Estate
> Stocks
> Annuities

This would also be a good time to re-emphasize the Defining Moments we have covered so far.

#1   Your money will never be worth more than
       it is today.

#2   This may be the lowest tax bracket you will ever
       be in.

#3   You cannot do the same things over and over again
       and expect different results.

#4   Learn what is true and what is not true.

#5   There are three types of money.

The transfers in your life can amount to a lot of money. Recapturing these transfers by reducing or eliminating them would allow you to keep more of your money. This could result in more options and opportunities in your life. Let's examine the ten most common transfers in people's lives.

1. Taxes

Taxes are the largest transfers in your financial life. The most common taxes are the income tax and social security tax. As part of the payroll tax, over the past several years, these taxes have not gone up much. The

Did you ever pay a tax you did not want to?

Did you ever pay a tax you did not have to?

other hundreds of taxes that don't make headlines continue to go up almost on an annual basis. In recent years, taxes have increased about 42% faster than personal incomes. State and local taxes have increased over 100% faster than national incomes. You now have to work five months of the year just to pay your taxes.

It is important to understand that with traditional thinking, we will continue to create and compound taxes for ourselves in the future. You cannot do the same things over and over again and expect different results. Everyone needs to understand that taxes are going to go up in the future, due to the demographic shifts in our country. Taxes will consume a majority of your future income.

2. Tax Refunds

Not only do we pay a lot of taxes, but also the average American has a tendency to overpay the taxes that are due. The IRS reports that the average refund for overpaying (paying too much) taxes is about $3,000. Getting a refund is not a victory. It is a mistake. With a $3,000 refund, it means that someone overpaid his or her taxes by about $250 a month. That is equal to a car payment per month. Does the Government credit interest or give you a dividend for giving them too much money? No. They get to use your money for almost a year – for free. You did get a thank-you letter from them, right? This is your money you are giving away and then you have to fight to get it back from them.

3. Qualified Plans

At best, qualified plans such as IRAs and 401Ks are forced savings programs. For most successful people, an IRA or 401K is not a tax savings event. A qualified plan simply defers the tax to a later date. A guarantee one should

When do you want to take money out of qualified plans?

When taxes are the lowest?

consider is that a qualified plan will be taxed at some point in time, and if invested in mutual funds or the stock market, the other guarantee is that the one investing in the plan is the only one at risk. When you retire, whatever you have

When will taxes be at their lowest?

Now or in the future?

accumulated in these plans will be taxed 20%, 30%, 40%, or more, regardless whether your investments did well or not. In the future, more thought should be given in utilizing qualified plans. Roth plans offer some relief for this dilemma, but qualified plans are not the only way to finance your future.

When you signed up for that 401K program, did you check the 30% or 40% guaranteed loss box?

4. Owning a Home

Purchasing a home, making mortgage payments, and owning a home that is paid off are events that are filled with multiple money transfers. When in the process of purchasing a home, there are title fees, escrow fees, filing fees, realtor fees, down payments, taxes, and many more. While you are making payments on your house, you pay interest rates, taxes on the property, insurance, maintenance costs, and improvements. When your home is paid for, you still have property taxes, insurance costs, and maintenance. There are a lot of decisions about the type of mortgage you should have. Most people want to live in the nicest house they can with the least amount of monthly payment, rather than the highest payment. Your home, mortgage, and equity are all tools that you should understand and learn how to use. There is an opportunity to recapture a lot of transfers you are experiencing in your home. Understand that the value of your home goes up or down, no matter how much equity you

> *What is the rate of return on your down payment?*
>
> Zero.

> *What is the rate of return on the equity in your house?*
>
> Zero.

> *Do you want to make the highest monthly payment or the lowest?*

have in your home. Interest rates, taxes, insurance, and a changing neighborhood can impact not only the value of your home but also the equity you have in it. The equity in your home when used properly can help you reduce other transfers occurring in your life. Never take the equity out of your home and invest it in the market.

Once again, our goal is to point out the transfers that impact your financial life. To get a more in-depth look at your approach to owning a home, read my book, *Learning To Avoid Unintended Consequences*, or request "Owning A Home, The Most Misunderstood American Dream" from the Wealth and Wisdom Institute, plus seek the help of a competent pro-fessional who is aware of the issues surrounding your home. Unfortunately, some financial companies disallow their representatives from having this conversation with the public. The lack of information and knowledge can only harm you.

5. Credit Cards

> A credit card balance of $5,000 at 18% interest will create $39,433 in interest payments over a 40-year period.

Today, the average American is carrying an enormous amount of debt. It is not uncommon to find credit card balances in the thousands of dollars. The marketing to the public from credit card companies is relentless. Credit cards have become part of our accepted culture, and along with it so are interest payments that are attached to them. The focus of many credit card companies is on late payments. They have reduced the number of billing days. That is the number of days you have to pay before the due date. You may also notice that many due dates are on a weekend. Plus, they still want you to allow them seven days to process your payment. All of this is to help the credit card company do one thing: to create a late payment from you and a $30 or $40 late fee for them.

Credit card debt is going to be some of the most expensive debt you can own. This causes major transfers in your life. Remember, in most cases, personal credit card debt interest is a non-deductible event when filing your taxes. By reducing the interest rates and restructuring your debt, you can recapture money that you are unknowingly and unnecessarily giving away.

6. Financial Planning

Depending on whom you talk to, financial planning can have many different faces. If you are talking to an investment broker, then stocks and mutual funds will be the center point of your planning. If you are talking to a real

> Did you ever get the feeling that the person you are discussing your finances with is one sale away from winning the company trip?

estate broker, then owning property is the only way to

go. If you are talking to an attorney, then the center point of the decision will be about will and trust and estate planning. If you are talking to a pension guru, then all you need to do is fund the heck out of your qualified plan. When you are seeking a direction for your future, amazingly, the recommendations that you get from someone will usually be the products that they sell. Some professionals charge fees for their advice, while others receive a commission for the products they sell. One way or another, they will be compensated for what they do. Remember, the professionals you deal with are paid whether they increase your wealth or lose some of it. These are just more transfers that you may be exposed to.

> *Someone tells you that he can get you a higher rate of return; who is the one at risk: you or the one making the recommendation?*

7. Investments

The vast majority of people are troubled and confused about the economy. They have been bombarded by the media, bullied by salespeople, and bewildered by the millions of things they feel they need to know. As discussed in this chapter, you can invest in bank savings programs, CDs, mutual funds, stocks, real estate,

> *Remember, you are the only one at risk!*

annuities, etc. All of these products expose you to some form of transfers of your wealth. The one thing you must understand is that owning a lot of different products does not make you smarter or better off financially.

8. Purchasing Cars

During your lifetime, let's say you purchased ten new cars starting at age 35. If you could have somehow just kept the interest you paid purchasing these cars and received a 7% rate of return on that money, you would have accumulated $576,473 by the time you reached the age of 79. After 40 years of driving, all you have to show for all that money is a four-year-old Buick worth about $8,000.

> A car is the greatest depreciating asset you will ever own.

What makes this transfer of your wealth so painful is that the interest you paid to the lending institutions for these cars is not tax-deductible. If you could somehow make all that interest tax-deductible, you would be able to recapture and keep some of the transfers you make from purchasing cars.

9. Life Insurance

> *If something has no value, do not insure it.*

A discussion about life insurance could go on and on forever. How much you should have and the types of policies you should own are major considerations. Typically, any conversation about life insurance is a conversation of avoidance. It is not fun to talk about. But, let's talk about the transfers in your life if you do not have life insurance. Your family's home, the lifestyle your family has become accustomed to, the children's education – all these may be in jeopardy in the event of your death. Let me ask you a question: If you found out that you qualified for two million dollars of life insurance from a life insurance company, how much coverage would you want? The most or the least? Now, let's say you found out you were dying. What do you feel your family deserves: the most or the least amount that you could offer them?

There are many ways life insurance contracts can play a major role in your life. The first lesson: do not die without one. It would end up being the largest transfer of wealth in your family's life.

10. Disability

> *48% of all home foreclosures are due to a disability.*

One of the most dramatic and unfortunate losses in life is one's inability to earn an income. Stop and think about this for a moment. You are working and earning a good living, paying your bills and taxes, and living very comfortably, and in one moment, you become disabled and lose the ability to pay for everything you have. How long can you live on your life savings before your lifestyle changes dramatically?

We spend our entire lives insuring others will get paid in the event something happens to us. We have mortgage insurance, liability insurance, hospitalization insurance, etc., to guarantee others will get paid. What about insuring <u>your</u> income so that <u>your</u> family will get paid? Transfers that occur from a disability will change someone's entire life, and it can become what I call "a living death."

Here & There

In this Defining Moment, The Three Types of Money, you need to learn the different types of money that flow into and out of your life. The power of your income will determine the type of lifestyle you will be able to afford. The transfers of your wealth starting with your income will reduce the amount of money you will be able to spend and save in the future.

Between where you are today financially and where you will ultimately end up at retirement are many obstacles and unintended consequences. Between here and there, you will be experiencing greater transfers of your wealth than you could ever imagine. These transfers will occur many times unknowingly and unnecessarily. These transfers will continue to happen throughout your entire life. Between here and there, you will also be confronted with other hazards that will impact your wealth. These hazards can be found in the changing demographics, investment and market risks, misinformation, taxation, government and personal debt, and finally, but most of all, a lack of fiscal knowledge that can be used in your everyday life. Between now and your financial future, if you do not recognize these hazards, you will continue to apply losing financial strategies and end up with a portfolio full of unintended consequences.

Learning how money works and learning how to recapture transfers of your wealth will help defend your financial future.

Defining Moment #6

Things You Can Do with Money

Now that you know that there are only three types of money in your life – lifestyle money, accumulated money, and transferred money – you probably won't be surprised to find out that there are only a few things that you can do with your money. You can simply spend it, save it, transfer it, or give it away. By far, your savings consumes the least amount of your money compared to the money that flows through your lifestyle money and money you simply transfer away. But, your ability or inability to save money receives more publicity than the other two types of money combined.

Being helpless, broke, and bald is not the way we should end up in life; it is how we begin life. The last couple of generations of Americans have developed an appetite for consuming goods well beyond their ability to pay for all the goods they have purchased. As a result, there is an enormous amount of personal debt in our country. This debt must be paid for with money that many have not earned yet. The pledging of future incomes to pay for debt leaves many in harm's way. Any interruption of income flow, rise in the cost of living, increased taxes, an illness, or an accident could leave the average American household in a desperate setting.

Understanding how money works and how money flows into and out of your life will help you control your personal finances more efficiently.

Spending Money

The consumer price index (CPI) measures the cost of buying goods and services for the average American. On a regular basis, 95,000 items from 22,000 stores are surveyed, and 35,000 rental-housing units are measured. The result concludes how the average American spends their money. According to the Social Security Administration, the breakdown of spending looks like this...

Housing	41.4%
Apparel	6.0%
Transportation	17.0%
Medical Care	6.9%
Entertainment	4.4%
Food & Beverage	17.4%
Other	6.9%

This looks fairly normal, but it should be noted that the housing figure is based on rental property and does not take into consideration the huge inflationary aspects of owning a home. Also, it should be pointed out that food and housing represent about 58% of the total. In addition, it is very important to understand that the average American pays more in taxes than they do for food and housing. The funny thing is that the CPI ignores the fact that we all must pay taxes and the cost of taxes is NOT included in the CPI. The cost of taxes eats up about 43% of our dollars. When the consumer price index is adjusted with taxes included, the average American's spending now looks like this...

Government (Fed, State & Local)	
Taxes	44.0%
Housing	23.0%
Food & Beverage	10.0%
Apparel	3.0%
Transportation	10.0%
Medical	4.0%
Entertainment	2.0%
Other	4.0%

Note that when taxes are included in our spending that more is spent on taxes than food, clothing, and housing combined by the average American. Because of taxes, the average person is limited on what he can spend on himself. Unfortunately, this also dramatically reduces the ability for someone to save money for the future (remember most attempts to save money for the future will also be taxed). Having less money to spend on our personal lives forces many average Americans into debt. The problem is, the government continues to outspend what the average consumer spends. This will create an even greater percentage of your money going to the government in the future.

There are marketing companies, financial institutions, and experts from the government who work 24/7 on new ways of separating YOU from your

MONEY. Spending money is easy, but remember, it takes more money to "play" than it does to work. By understanding how your money flows out of your life via transfers, you can now focus on the problem you face instead of chasing another quick fix, marketing scheme. You must understand that the solution is not difficult. It is based on logic and knowledge. It is time to take a stand against the money changers of the world.

When thinking about your spending habits and learning the Defining Moments, the goal is not to have you go through life without the lifestyle you deserve. It is quite the opposite. Learning how your money works will afford you almost all the things you ever wanted. Your spending should be proportionate not to just your income but the amount of your income you are allowed to keep. Therefore, the solution to some of the financial problems you face is not your income but rather to reduce or eliminate the transfers of wealth you experience in your everyday life that reduces the amount of income you are allowed to keep. Do not make the mistake of believing that the amount of credit you have for spending is an amount you can safely afford above and beyond your income.

Saving Money

Compared to spending money, saving money is much more difficult. More of our time and attention is focused on spending our money. Very little time is centered on saving. The last two generations of Americans have drifted away from taking some amount of their incomes and saving it. If you were paying attention, there was not a category in the consumer price index (CPI) for savings. Savings in the United States have plummeted to an all-time low. This is amazing when you factor in that many households have two income earners. Still, over the past few years, consumers found it necessary to draw down their savings just to maintain their lifestyles and to make up for the declining buying power of their incomes. This is occurring at the same time when there are significant negative trends in company benefits and pensions, health insurance, social security, and dramatic increases in government spending that will result in higher personal taxes. The Government Accountability Office (GAO) reported recently that personal savings were at a negative rate in our country. The spending and costs needed to maintain an average family's lifestyle robs them of any opportunity to personally save money. It is ironic that the government has secured its future through your income with no regard to your financial survival in your future. Any attempt you make to save money for your future must be shared with the government.

> *Over the last few years, consumers have found it necessary to draw down their savings just to maintain their lifestyles and to make up for the declining buying power of their incomes.*

Saving is not just physically putting money somewhere and hoping it will grow. Saving is also NOT spending money you do not have to, unknowingly and unnecessarily. Understanding this type of saving and recapturing transfers of your wealth will help you save the money you are simply giving away. The process, the way you spend your money, is filled with opportunities for others (banks, credit card companies, mortgage companies, the government, etc.) to make money FROM you, not FOR YOU. What they market as a savings for you is really a profit for them. The funny thing is none of these companies have money until you give it to them.

Americans have not saved so little since the Great Depression in the 1930s. They are on a spending binge well beyond the growth of their incomes.

So, your personal savings can be a combination of two elements: the actual money you can save and the money you do not have to spend (fees, taxes, interest rates, etc.) in your everyday life.

Choice and Chance

What many people do not understand is that there is a difference between "savings" and "investments," and in today's traditional thinking, it can cause many problems. Savings is money that you have accumulated and you want that money to grow in value but with very little, if not any, risk. This should be money that you can count on to be there for retirement or whenever you need it. With the continued onset of government programs such as social security,

Medicare, and Medicaid, the average American is lulled into a false sense of security that they do not have to save any money because these government programs provide a safety net for them in the future. The problem is that these programs are not free. The government continues to try to fix their social dream programs of the 1960s. These programs, if left unchanged, will bankrupt America. The average American dependency on the government is now at a crossroad. Does the government do something now to save America and cut back on its spending and cut government benefits by 60% OR simply double the taxes we are currently paying and hope for the best? In a world that is filled with overwhelming challenges, everyone must re-learn how to save money.

The difference between savings and investments is the word RISK. I will give you an example. Many politicians do not want you to have control to invest some of your social security account into investments because it is A.) too risky, or B.) they think you are too dumb to do it. (Just a side note here: the real reason they do not want you to be able to invest some of your social security payments is that they, the government, would now be accountable for your account and they would not be able to spend this money for other things and that would mess up their lives.) The funny thing is that the government does not think it is too risky to put all your money into 401Ks or IRAs that involve investing. While contemplating on investing, remember one thing, YOU ARE THE ONLY ONE AT RISK. The tradeoff for "trying" or "hoping" for higher rates of returns is the fact that you COULD possibly lose "a little," or "some," or "a lot" of your money. For many, social security has become their savings, and 401Ks, IRAs, and other retirement plans have become supplements for retirement income.

As it is for savings, finding money from your income to set aside for investments is becoming more difficult. Accumulating money through investments has become the most popular way of attempting to increase one's wealth, yet it remains the most misunderstood. Remember, it is far more important to understand how money works than what it is invested in. You should begin the practice of separating your savings from your investments.

> *Your economic situation is a matter of choice, not a matter of chance.*

Now That I Am Saving Money...

If you have been fortunate enough to save money, now what do you do with it? Well, the goal may be to let it just ACCUMULATE. Everyone wants their money to grow. You could also FLATTEN your savings and investments. Flattening means that you keep the basis (what you originally invested or saved) intact and take only the money that you have earned from your accounts and take it as income every year. The goal of flattening is to keep the basis or principle of your accounts at the same level while drawing income from them. This would allow you to never run out of income-bearing money in the future.

You could also decide to SPEND DOWN an asset or your savings. Spending down an asset is withdrawing money from an account until the balance of the account is gone. As an example, if someone had $100,000 and wanted to SPEND DOWN that entire amount over a ten-year period, and while they were spending it down, they received a 5% rate of return on the balance that was still in the account, they would receive $12,333.17 per year for ten years. At the end of ten years, there would be no money left. If someone were to FLATTEN out this same $100,000 account with a 5% annual rate of return, this person would receive $4,761.90 per year and the account balance would remain at $100,000 at the end of each year. At retirement, you will make decisions on whether to let your money continue to ACCUMULATE or whether to FLATTEN out or SPEND DOWN what you have saved during your life.

So far, we have discussed how you spend your money and also the difference between savings and investments. We have also looked at how your savings will be used. Whether you let your savings simply accumulate or use it for income by flattening out or spending down will be determined by you and the economic situation you are in. Your savings will create financial opportunities for you during your entire life, not just your retirement years. Learning to spend down or flatten out an asset could help you achieve goals that you may have now and in the future. By understanding these spending and saving concepts, you will start to see how your money works…for you.

Transfernation

As a nation, we have become very good at spending money and pretty pathetic at saving it. As a nation, the average American has developed some bad habits in the way we buy things and conduct our personal financial lives. The convenience of credit and the perceived nuisance of paying cash create unnecessary fees and charges in our everyday lives. Not only do we pay for the goods on credit but also all the taxes charged for purchasing those goods. That is right, think of all the taxes that can be charged on a credit card. Everyone is constantly being brainwashed that the only way to purchase everything is by using credit. It is important to remember the definition of lost opportunity cost. When you spend a dollar, not only do you lose that dollar but also the ability to earn money from that dollar. When you purchase something, at least you have the goods or services you purchased. Lost opportunity cost also applies to transfers of your wealth. When you spend money for taxes, fees, charges, and interest, not only do you lose those dollars but again the ability to earn money from those dollars. The problem is when you pay for those transfers, you get no goods in exchange for your money. It is not uncommon for the average family to give away $500 or more PER MONTH.

It is possible that by examining how you spend, save, and transfer or give away money that you can recapture dollars that are flowing out of your life today. To recapture these dollars, you are not exposed to market risks, taxes, fees, or interest rates. You will be surprised that in recapturing these dollars that you will not spend a single penny more than you are spending right now to do this.

Other than the most obvious transfers of your wealth such as income taxes, mortgage interest, and credit card costs, I could probably rattle off another two hundred transfers that you are exposed to either directly or indirectly, in your everyday life. It is important to find an experienced trained professional to uncover and recapture the dollars that you have become accustomed to giving away. Recapturing these dollars will enable you to spend and save more of your money.

The average American is under the impression that in order to save money that he must give up some of his worldly goods. After all, how much time would you want to spend in reducing your lifestyle to save for the future? Probably not much time at all. But, if you can save money by reducing and recapturing transfers and not spend any additional money, would you do it? This is the power of understanding how money works.

So, what can you do with your money? Well, you can spend it. Go ahead and have a good time and improve your life, but do not spend more than you make. You can save money. This is harder than spending it. Remember, there is a difference between "savings" and investments. Savings cannot only be real money you save but also money you do not give away (transfers). Once you save money, you can let it accumulate, "flatten it out" or "spend it down" and use it for income or purchases. Finally, we unfortunately give away a lot of money through transfers of wealth in our everyday lives. Some of these transfers are controllable and can be recaptured. Recapturing these dollars can add up to a lot of money. Controlling this money will increase your ability to save money and improve your financial future. All of this can be accomplished without spending one more dime than you are already spending.

Defining Moment #7

There is good debt;
there is bad debt.

When it comes to debt, everyone should pay attention, otherwise you will be paying others for the rest of your life. Debt is a tool, not a convenience. It should be taken seriously. Your credit has been made convenient for you to use on a daily basis. Your credit availability has been established from the amount of your income, your ability to pay, and your credit and debt history. While examining your credit worthiness, banks and lending institutions will classify you in one of two categories. You will be viewed as a creditor or a debtor. A creditor is someone that when given a loan has the financial ability to pay off the loan whenever he wants. A debtor is a person that when given a loan has every intention to pay that loan off but not necessarily right away. If you are a creditor, you may receive favorable interest rates from lending institutions. If you are a debtor, your opportunities may be limited. You may have to pay more for the use of "someone else's money" (SEM). Excessive debt will impact your ability to receive any additional credit, and in a credit frenzy society, this could make life difficult. Don't ever feel a bank or lending institution has done you a favor in lending you money. They will profit from you...every opportunity they can, without shame. Heaven help you if you are ever late with a payment, even just once. In the fine print, your tardiness allows them to stain your credit history, raise your interest rate, charge you additional outrageous fees, and jeopardize the interest rates you have with other lenders. The fine print was designed by a large team of high-priced lawyers to defend the bank from you and then punish you as severely as the law will allow them. The scariest words from a lending institution are "don't worry, signing these forms will just take a minute and you'll be on your way." In addition to purchasing the goods you wanted when you signed these papers, you unknowingly started a series of events that could change your financial life.

> *A bank is someone who will lend you an umbrella when it's not raining, and wants it back when it does.*

It is unfortunate that our politicians and representatives, who have been elected to help defend us against harm, allow financial companies to charge interest rates to the public that are 20%, 30%, and 40% higher than the prime interest rates. Millions of Americans have pledged their future incomes not just to purchase everyday goods but also homes, cars, and their kids' educations. In today's world, credit is not an option; it is almost a must.

When debt is created, it is everyone's intention to pay it off. Unfortunately, there are events in life that we don't control. Almost half of all foreclosures of houses today

> *If you think you can borrow your way to prosperity ...think again.*

are caused when there is a disability and a loss of income in a household. It is becoming more common that the loss of a job, an illness, a divorce, or a death leads to a path of financial disaster because of debt. No matter what happens, the debt payment is due. When it comes to your credit and debt, be proactive, not reactive.

The Dues and Don'ts of Debt

The debt you accumulate further reduces your ability to save and purchase other goods in your lifestyle. Not only is the principle payment due, but also the interest along with account fees, processing fees, and possible late fees. Remember, most of these payments flow out of your lifestyle and are paid with after-tax dollars. We have also discussed that once you spend a dollar, you also lose the ability to earn money on that dollar you spent. These are all transfers of your wealth. Financial institutions understand Defining Moment number one very clearly: Money will never be worth more than it is today. They want as much of your money as they can possibly get, as soon as they can get it. To avoid these pitfalls of debt, there are things you should do and shouldn't do when it comes to debt.

> *Money now is worth more than money later.*

DON'T JUST PAY DEBT, MANAGE IT. Avoid accumulating debt that is beyond your income capabilities. Be aware of the life-changing events that could disrupt your income flow. If possible, insure yourself that your debt can be paid in the event of disability or death.

DON'T BE LATE WHEN PAYING. If you are late in paying off debt, you could find the consequences uncomfortable. Making late payments could trigger higher interest rates, late fees, and a reduced credit score. The aftereffects of late payments can haunt you for years. If you are going to be late with a payment, call the company. Some attempt to discuss your payment is better than avoiding the issues. Payment management is important.

DON'T SIGN UP FOR CREDIT CARDS AT A STORE REGISTER. You are getting ready to pay for some clothes you picked out and the clerk informs you that you can save another 20% on your purchase if you sign up today for their credit card. Don't do it. You don't have time to read or discuss the "fine print" of what you're agreeing to if you sign up. Having too many credit cards isn't a victory in your financial world.

A PURCHASE BECOMES PART OF YOUR REAL DEBT IF YOU DON'T PAY IT OFF IN 30 DAYS. Many Americans make casual purchases on a daily basis with credit cards. These casual purchases become real debt and a part of your monthly budget if they are not paid in full in 30 days.

DON'T CONTINUOUSLY "FLIP" CREDIT CARDS. What looks like short-term relief of credit card interest rates and monthly payments by constantly changing credit card companies creates some unintended consequences. This constant activity on your credit report reveals not a credit strength but a credit weakness. Inquiries by companies for your credit scores can also create red flags on your credit report.

DON'T FINANCE YOUR HOME TO THE MAX. The equity in your home can be a valuable tool when used for the right reasons. The equity in your home can act as your own personal safety net. It is important to have access to your equity, but not misuse it. The equity could be viewed as if it were a bank for you – but, and read this clearly, not an investment account. Mortgage rates, property tax rates, insurance rates, an unstable housing market, and inflation can play havoc with the value of a home. When contemplating a mortgage, refinancing, or establishing an equity line of credit, confide in a financial professional other than the companies who are willing to lend you the money. Personally, my equity line of credit is an active financial option in my life, but is under control at all times.

IN SOME CASES, PAYING CASH IS NOT ALWAYS THE BEST OPTION. Your money will never be worth more than it is today. Sometimes, controlling cash (today's money) is more valuable than paying cash and losing the ability to earn money from that money. Everyone should enjoy living in the nicest house and driving the nicest car one can for the least amount of monthly payment, not the most monthly payment.

LEARN TO SAVE. Having savings at hand will change your credit and debt life. Saving additional money can be difficult with all the financial stress the average American faces. Learning to reduce debt and the costs and fees that go along with debt could create the savings you need in your financial life. This can be done without spending one more dime than you are already spending.

BECOME A CREDITOR, NOT A DEBTOR. A lending institution will take note that if you're looking for a loan that you have savings, investments, and other accounts that convince the lender that you are in control of your finances. If you go into a bank totally broke, that is the way you will leave. For someone who needs a loan but has very little control of his finances, he will be classified as a debtor by the lender and may have to pay higher interest rates and fees. Don't go into a financial institution begging for money.

There Is Good Debt. . .

As our grandparents would have us believe, not all debt is bad debt. Using someone else's money (SEM) is not a bad thing for purchasing a house or a car. Using debt could allow some families to maintain their lifestyle even while sending Junior to college. Unfortunately, except for mortgage interest, interest that is paid on most other loans is not deductible from your federal taxes. Some borrowers may elect to take a loan for a purchase even though they have enough money and savings to pay cash for the goods. They may feel that the rate of return they are receiving on their savings is greater than the interest rate they will pay for the loan. If debt can create real value in your life and you can financially control it and not have it control you, then use it. Remember though, the interest you pay is a transfer of your wealth.

You may have a financial tool available to you that you haven't considered. If you own a home, it is possible that you have accumulated a lot of equity. When borrowed, the equity interest you pay will most likely be tax-deductible. The IRS has some limitations, but your equity can be a powerful borrowing tool. Imagine borrowing money for your child's education and having the interest you paid become tax-deductible. Imagine borrowing money for a new car and being able to deduct the interest paid. Depending on the interest rate, this would be far better than not deducting the interest payment. Imagine receiving a tax refund on the interest you have paid. Receiving the deduction is recapturing a wealth transfer that you were otherwise simply giving away.

Leverage

When it comes to your purchases, savings, and investments, one of the most important thought processes that needs to be developed is centered on the word LEVERAGE. The idea of leverage is this: You want to use the least amount of today's dollars to gain the most amount of value in the future. Donald Trump would never pay cash for a piece of property he wants. He would give up the least amount of his money to gain control of the property, borrow the rest, and manage that property to create value. Where in Donald Trump's thought process is the phrase "and pay it off as fast as I can"? Mr. Trump knows that his money will never be worth more than it is today. He knows that keeping as much of his money as he can will make him rich, not the bank or mortgage company. He also understands that making more payments on that property later rather than sooner is important. He knows, due to inflation, a thousand dollars today will have the buying power of four hundred and eleven dollars thirty years from now because of a three percent inflation rate. Why are the banks and mortgage companies telling their clients to do the complete opposite and pay the most they can sooner, rather than later? It is because they also understand that money has more buying power today than tomorrow.

There are very few things in your life that you purchase that create leverage. Most of the goods an average American buys depreciate over time, lose value, and need to be replaced. A home, a business, and a life insurance policy are examples of things that you can purchase with the least amount of today's dollars that could create the most amount of future value for you or your family. Not only do these assets have real value, but you are also the one who owns and controls them. In many ways, you determine the value of these assets. These assets can also become financial tools for you in the future and can be used as collateral financially. Your home, business, and insurance are probably the largest assets that you will pass on to your family.

Well, what about. . .

Someone is going to ask what about investing money in the markets. Just about everyone, including me, invests money into stocks or mutual funds. When you invest one dollar, it is in the hope that it will go up in value and continue to grow. The problem is, there is nothing you can do, no control, to make that fund or stock grow. There is no way to drive them forward to make more money. There is also no hard asset, like a house or a business, behind mutual funds or stocks. You can improve your home and business and make the value increase while you are using them for shelter and income. You can also buy more insurance for pennies on the dollar, thus increasing the legacy for your family. Don't get me wrong, I think investing in solid stocks or funds is good, but are typically not purchases with outcomes that you have some ability to control.

The reason I'm bringing this up is that I would not have a problem borrowing money to improve my house or business, but I would have a problem borrowing money to invest in stocks or mutual funds. If someone did borrow money to invest in the market, he would face the interest he must pay for borrowing the money, the risk of down markets, fees, and taxation on any growth in value. To me, that is too many negatives to face in an attempt to increase value. Remember, LEVERAGE is the attempt to use the LEAST amount of money to gain the most value, control, and security in your life. I would rather learn to make one dollar do the work of ten instead of trying to make ten dollars earn the value of one...LEVERAGE.

Then There Is Bad Debt

The "I'll figure it out tomorrow" crowd is in serious trouble when it comes to personal and family finance. Our society is filled with a whole generation of "I want it now" thinkers who live on the very edge of financial collapse. Financial debt causes more depresssion, desperation, and divorce in our country than anything. Debt ratios are tearing the very social fabric of our society. Bad debt can be caused by a lack of will, knowledge, or just simply bad luck. No matter what the excuse, the result is the same. The debt must be paid. Americans buy things on credit that go out of style, break, and don't work, or end up in a garage sale before it is paid off. Personal debt ratios have increased much faster than personal incomes and savings. A large dose of reality will impact our entire country if changes about personal and government debt don't occur soon. The next generation of Americans face the possibility of becoming the first generation of Americans to have a declining standard of living. Many Americans are in the mode of controlled failure.

In many cases, bad debt can be overcome with the use of knowledge and common sense. No one is holding a gun to your head and saying buy, buy, buy. Yes, it is getting more difficult to save, invest, and maintain your lifestyle because the forces around you have changed and you haven't. The Defining Moments will give you a base for your everyday financial lives. Along with outspending incomes, the focus should be on other transfers that cause financial uncertainty in your life. These are situations that you can learn to control.

Defining Moment #8

Rich people think. . .
Poor people think. . .

How many opportunities have passed you by because you weren't aware of them? What you know and the way you think TODAY will impact your financial future more than anything. Many times, the average American is willing to rely more on risk and chance than knowledge when it comes to their money. What is curious is how rich families seem to continually remain rich generationally, even though the investment choices, stocks, mutual funds, real estate, etc., are the same for everyone, whether rich or poor. Now, I know I made that sound somewhat simplistic, but think about it for a second. Everyone will wake up tomorrow with the same opportunity to invest in the same stocks or funds and get the same rate of return – whether they are rich, middle class, or poor. So, there is no real advantage in the types of investments, only the opportunity for the rich to invest more. If picking the right investments was the only difference between the rich and the poor, then the poor would only have to mimic the investment decisions of the rich.

So, what is the difference between the rich and the poor? What do these families do that other families don't do? It's the thought process. For the rich, the center of their financial life is their family and/or business. These center points of their lives are things they own and control. When it comes to their thinking, the rich have three basic rules when it comes to finances. Rule one: Use the least amount of money to create the most amount of wealth. Rule two: Guarantee the wealth will occur and a legacy will transfer tax-free. Rule three: Create multiples of wealth immediately. These three rules of the rich are quite different than the average American's approach to his typical 401K. Traditional thinking would have you invest in the stock market, real estate, qualified plans, and bank savings vehicles. None of these traditional investments meet the three rules of the rich.

The traditional thinking that the average American is exposed to also contains some wealth transfers. Possible market losses, account and management fees, income taxes, capital gains taxes, maintenance costs, and possible estate tax implications all reduce your wealth. As years go by, these transfers accumulate to a large sum of money. Now just think, if you could keep these transfers of your wealth and earn five or six percent on that money, it would dramatically compound your wealth.

Although most Americans will prosper and have a good life financially, it pales in comparison had they had the knowledge to apply the rules of the rich to their lives. The center point of most traditional thinking is focused on home ownership and the 401K thought process. Don't get me wrong, I believe owning a

> ## Rule # 1
>
> Use the least amount of money to create the most amount of wealth.

home and saving for retirement are really good things, but it is not the only financial thought process you should have. Remember, you need to be aware of the transfers that are associated with home ownership and retirement plans.

So, while most Americans aspire to be rich, the only thing stopping them from being rich is knowing the thought process and refocusing the center points of their financial lives. Rich people think like rich people; poor people think like poor people.

If you knew something was going to be given to you in the future, would you want it to grow in value, or would you let it sit there and lose its value? If you could do something to increase the value of what was going to be given to you with a small investment on your part, would you do it? If you could "make" the value grow two, three, or four times what it is worth today and use the least amount of your money, would you do it? While you're at it, if you could make it tax-free when it came to you, would you want that to happen also? If you could insure and guarantee all of this to happen, would you do it? If you could do all of this without spending any more money than you're already spending today, would you do it? This is what the rich do. Does this sound like a 401K? An IRA? An investment portfolio? A bank savings account?

> **Rule # 2**
>
> *Guarantee the wealth will occur and the legacy will transfer tax-free.*

> **Rule # 3**
>
> *Create multiples of wealth immediately.*

If you are really rich, a real concern would be the amount of taxation the government would seize from everything you owned and worked for your entire life should you die. Current law states that the estate tax will be phased out. In order to keep it phased out, the Congress will have to renew the law in 2010. If they don't renew the law, the estate tax is back in play. Understanding the government's need for revenue and how "taxing the rich" seems to please those running for public office, it seems that some form of estate tax will be there in the future. Depending on when you are reading this, the estate tax law could have already changed. To explain how the rich avoid this estate taxation, I must describe it in the form of a "fairy tale." The lesson here is not whether the numbers are correct or not but rather the thought process that is used.

Once upon a time, there were some rich folks. This family consisted of a father, mother, and a couple of kids. The father and mother had great careers, and over a period of time they accumulated a large net worth. Ten million bucks! They knew that if they were to die, they would owe the king about four million dollars in taxes. One day the king proclaimed to the rich family that if they gifted all their worldly goods to charities within the kingdom when they died, that he would grant them a charitable foundation. The king would also grant them tax credit now, while they were alive, for doing this. With these tax credits, the father and mother would insure their lives for ten million bucks when they died. Their kids would be the beneficiaries of ten million dollars tax-free. By doing this, the rich family preserved all of the family wealth, and passed it on to the next generation tax-free. They all lived happily ever after. The End.

The rich understand the wealth transfers that they face in their lives and work hard to avoid them. Avoiding wealth transfers that they face in the future allows them to spend more of their money today. You may not have many things in common with rich people, but what you do have in common is the ability to view your family as a very valuable tool. Now go back and read the little fairy tale again and look for one thing you could do to invest back into your family.

How can you say yes or no to ideas that you don't even know exist?

The rich know the value of financial tools. They realize that their family is one of the most valuable financial tools that they have. To underestimate the wealth potential of the family in the future is a grave miscalculation. To the average American, understanding that the family is a financial tool isn't even a consideration in their thought process. This is the difference between the rich and the poor. Unfortunately, without knowledge, this will never change.

If saving money in your life is a problem, concentrate on the wealth transfers in your life to solve the problem. If creating multiples of wealth in your future is desirable, focus on your family, all of your family, as a financial tool. If

It is difficult to find the right solution when you start out with the wrong premise.

you believe as I do, that the taxes in your future will

eliminate much of your future income, your family as a financial tool could solve the problem. This is not about a will or a trust, although those are important. This is about increasing family value and learning how it can change your life. To discover how to view your family as a financial tool and how this could impact and change your life, seek out a trusted advisor or educator who can discuss all of the opportunities available.

By understanding all of the Defining Moments we have discussed so far, you should begin to notice how they interact with each other. The goal is to develop a thought process that will aid you in making better life decisions. The Defining Moment will also free you from some of the pitfalls of traditional thinking.

Creating Real Life Value

For many of us, we have been trained or brainwashed into thinking that the only solution to our financial success is purchasing and owning the right financial products. But, the real answer to controlling wealth is knowledge and the thought process. If all the products one can purchase are the same for the rich and for the poor, then the product is not the difference between the rich or middle class. The difference must be the thought process and knowing how money works. The reality is that the average American does not pay enough attention to his financial life simply because he doesn't know how to. He fixes his financial life by switching products and hoping for better results. Remember Defining Moment number three: You can't do the same things over and over and expect different results.

Many people have thoughts but don't know how to think. They believe that changing their financial thought process would be a monumental chore. Understanding the defining moments will allow you to take small steps now to create large rewards later while learning a process that will impact your everyday thinking. People need to understand that there is a difference between simply living your life and building a life. To improve your life, start asking yourself these questions: What did I learn today? What did I improve today? What did I accomplish today? First, to be successful financially, you must have a philosophy that will strengthen your financial position. Second, have a strategy that you understand and control, and finally, learn your financial solutions might be right in front of you.

There will always be different levels of rich, middle class, and poor people. It is possible that the actions we take today will improve or decrease our financial value in the future. What is more important: knowing how money works or having a balanced portfolio? It is equally important to understand the financial tools that are available to you in your financial world and everyday life. These are the things that you may never have thought of before. But, how can you be aware of opportunities that you didn't even know existed? Rich people think like rich people, and that will never change. The rules of the rich are based on common sense and logic. The rest of the people think differently, but that can change, and everyone can adapt to the thought process of the rich. It is time to reach out beyond the walls of traditional thinking.

Defining Moment #9

The Goals for Financial Success

When you apply the first eight Defining Moments to your everyday life, you will experience a financial change that you will be able to feel and see. The Defining Moments in your life will not take years to develop. You will start to see financial changes very quickly. The results of applying the Defining Moments to your life will help you achieve the four basic goals:

1. You will increase your money supply.
2. You will create more or better benefits for you and your family.
3. You will reduce the element of risk when trying to increase your wealth and also reduce the amount of future taxation you face.
4. Achieve these three goals without spending one more dime than you are already spending.

Developing a philosophy and a thought process using the Defining Moments will point you to the goals you can achieve. These goals are the result of controlling your money and understanding how money works.

Money

Having money is essential in almost every aspect of life. For those who have it, or are rich, they feel a certain sense of security. When you have money, you have the luxury of worrying about other things in life. For those who have very little or no money, you live in a different world. A business without money has very little chance of surviving, even charities. In fact, most businesses fail in their early years due to a lack of capital. In many American households, it's no different. In a family setting, a lack of money or large amounts of debt can bring a family to its knees. Many times the financial troubles in a family can result in depression, desperation, or divorce. This impacts the social fabric of our society and creates secondary problems like crime, drugs, and a lack of education. The lack of money creates dependency on the government, which is not supposed to be in the family business. Any way you look at it, a lack of money has the ability to strip individuals and families of their pride and sense of self-worth. Many Americans also have the fear of knowing that they may be only two or three paychecks away from being broke.

> *Many times your economic situation is a matter of choice, not chance.*

For many, not having the sufficient cash flow to live a comfortable life is due to a series of financial decisions that they made in the past. These decisions cause problems financially and have a compounding impact in their life today and into the future. This is why I have chosen to focus on the "money supply" of an individual or family first. Having a money supply and having the ability to increase that money supply are far more important than investing in a stock tip, and they have better results.

Increasing Your Money Supply

To increase the money supply in your life, you will not have to change the way you live your life, only the way you approach life financially. Everyone should learn the defining moments and pay attention in their daily lives when it comes to their money. The answers for improving your financial life are right in front of you. You need to be more reactive when you see an opportunity to improve your money supply.

In Defining Moment #5, we discussed the three types of money, and in Defining Moment #6, the things you can do with money. Both of those lessons include a discussion about the transfers of your wealth. This is money that you unknowingly and unnecessarily may be giving away. Transfers of your wealth rob you of your ability to save money, invest, or improve your lifestyle. Recapturing the money you're transferring away now will increase your money supply. If you are able to keep this money now, it will compound the amount of wealth you will have in the future.

Some financial thought processes you had in the past will have to change, nothing else, not the car you drive, the house you live in, or your vacations. If you can increase your money supply by just changing a thought, would you do it? You may need to rethink the way you're buying your house, paying for your car, or the way you manage debt. You may need to rethink the way you're saving for retirement, your 401K, your investments. You also may need to rethink the way you buy things and pay for them. If your home is paid off, you may want to examine options you have. You see, to have the ability to increase your money supply right now, all you have to do is think. It will be important to discuss these issues with a professional who has been educated regarding the transfers of your wealth. [See the back of this book for the type of professional who has been trained to have these discussions with you.] Once you have discovered that you can increase your money supply now, make the necessary changes and simply keep more of your money. Having more money will change the way you think, feel, and live.

Making decisions today can increase your money supply, but in order to maintain that money supply you will need to be aware of the impact that the demographic changes in our country will have on you financially. If you're successful in your life or live a comfortable life. . . taxes will go up. Due to inflation, your buying power will go down; costs will continue to rise, and benefits you thought you would have may disappear. This is not a doomsday scenario but a fact. You must understand that the cost of government must go up. About forty percent of incomes in America rely on government jobs. These workers get pay increases and benefits. On top of that, the government continues to spend more than they take in.

Once you increase your money supply by recapturing transfers, you will need to pay attention and possibly rethink what to do with this money. There is no sense using the same traditional thinking with this newfound money that created transfers in the first place. Defining Moment #3, you can't do the same things over and over again and expect different results. Learn what is true and what may not be true, Defining Moment #4, when it comes to developing a new thought process in your life. You will be amazed how much of your money is being given away simply to benefit others.

When looking to invest the recaptured money you now control, look to the things around you, the things closest to you. Look at the wealth potential and life value of your family, your whole family, grandparents and parents included. Look at investing in your business or using the money to increase your lifestyle. All of these issues – your family, your business, and your lifestyle

Don't go to a foot doctor if you have a headache.

– are things that you control. Family inheritances are something that should not happen by accident. They should be discussed, planned, controlled, and leveraged to create the greatest amount of family wealth. With proper planning, much of the family wealth avoids future taxation to the next generation. Remember, taxes are and will be the largest transfer in everyone's life. Working with a strong loving family is a financial tool no one should overlook. Get professional help when discussing family opportunities and creating family wealth. Simply establishing a will or a trust doesn't create family wealth; it is simply an attempt to protect the wealth that is already there. Don't be confused by this point. Wills and trusts are important, but it is not a plan to strategically increase family wealth. So, it is important to also look beyond an accountant or a lawyer for a professional who can have these discussions with you. Look for the right answers, not the simply generic ones. Whatever you do, recapturing transfers will create more freedom to do the things you want to do in life and more control to do them. There will be less financial pressure and a greater ability to enjoy the best life you can right now.

Since this book was designed to be an educational tool and make you think, you may want to review lost opportunity costs (LOC) and liquidity, use, and control (LUC) of your money that were discussed earlier in this book. These lessons teach you the value of "today's" money. Your mind is somewhat like a computer. If you put bad software in your computer or allow a virus to infect all your programs, then the computer will be of little use. Your mind is the same way. If you fill it with basic information, you are going to get basic results. Too many people are sold on the "get rich, it's easy" schemes and the "everyone can get rich in the marketplace" thought process. Unfortunately, very few take the time to learn and understand how money works in their everyday lives.

Once again, the inability to save money by the average American is a major concern. Over a period of time, the lack of savings will stop economic growth in our country. Much of today's economic growth can be attributed to a tremendous increase in personal consumer debt. More than any point in our country's history has debt been so large. Over the last few years, more Americans have dipped into their savings just to pay their everyday lifestyle bills. Hopefully, you can sense and feel the value of reducing transfers in your life and increasing your money supply.

Creating More Benefits

Creating and understanding ways of increasing your money supply will give you options and opportunities in your life. There are many things in your life that you probably want to do and many things that you should do to improve your quality of life. Unfortunately, many of the things you should and want to do are simply not affordable. Benefits are often thought of as something you receive at work, such as medical coverage, disability coverage, and a retirement plan. In today's world, more and more of these benefits are disappearing or are provided with some expense to the worker. These benefits are good things, but their costs continue to increase. More and more families are "going without" or "reducing" their benefits because of affordability. The government's own accountability office warns that social benefits provided by the Federal Government may have to be reduced by as much as 60% because they are no longer affordable. The GAO considers the overall direction of the government's financial position as a "crisis" with no real exit strategy. Relying on government programs, as we now know them, to be there in the future is the wrong platform to plan your future. Creating and controlling our money supply will help you provide the security and protection you and your family will need in the future.

There is an odd thought process that has filtered throughout our society. A benefit is a great thing UNLESS you are the one who has to pay for it. As an example, let's say tomorrow when you get to work, your company notifies you that they will provide and pay for one million dollars of life insurance coverage for you and your family as a benefit. All you have to do is say yes to receive the benefit. That's great. That benefit assures your family a future, a means of not only surviving, but also maintaining the lifestyle they now enjoy, in the event of your death. What is the price of financial security? You willingly sign up for the benefit. Nine months later the company changes its mind about providing this benefit, but they say you can keep the coverage if YOU pay for it. The cost is $1,000 per year. You're upset and tell the company that you're not paying anything. Why, in the course of one company memo, did the coverage for your family go from a great idea to an idea that wasn't worth doing?

Providing the traditional benefits, health care, disability, etc. for you and your family are important. By increasing your money supply and reducing your wealth transfers, other benefits begin to surface. Doing the things you want to do in life, increasing your quality of life, taking vacations, traveling, securing education for your children, creating a family legacy, having financial control and financial security – all are benefits of increasing your money supply. With these secondary benefits come a healthy, less stress-prone future and the time freedom, money freedom, and control you need to live the best life you can.

Reducing Risk

Certain types of risk should only be taken when necessary. A definition of risk is simply this: uncertain results. We take risks every day. We drive, cross streets, and tell our wives we're going out with the boys on a Saturday night. With these types of risks, we have some amount of control. We can be extra careful driving and crossing the street and come home early with flowers. When it comes to your finances, risks can be more difficult to control.

When investing, risk is usually associated with the rate of return, or potential outcome, you will receive. Like driving or crossing the street, if you are unaware of the potential dangers, investing is subject to accidents or a crash could occur, and in one brief moment, your life could change.

As you get older, you move from the accumulation stage of your life to the preservation stage during retirement. Someone who is retired and continues to leave all his money exposed to risks in the stock market could be playing a reckless game with lady luck. The risks are not just the ups and downs of the market but also the value of the dollar, tax increases, and a terrorist attack that would create financial instability. None of these risks are controlled by you. Once again, as mentioned earlier in this book, you need to understand the difference between your "savings" and your "investments."

Unfortunately, you will be surrounded and flooded with marketing from financial companies continuing to follow the traditional thought processes. It is important to remember their solution to your financial problems will always be the products they sell. Many times these solutions (product choices) will constantly change from year to year. Sometimes planners' solutions are so complicated that within a week you can't remember or explain what or how your stock plan works. One rule of thumb when involving yourself with a planner, make sure he owns the same investments he is recommending to you. Not knowing or understanding your investments' strategy is a risk in itself.

The uncertainty of future tax increases is another risk that will eat away a large portion of your future dollars. It is almost a certainty that future taxes on your money must go up. Even the Government Accountability Office (GAO) states on their website that in order to survive as a nation, future taxes will have to double from the current rates we are paying. Our country's declining workforce, aging population, and increasing benefits point to one thing: higher taxes. Everyone in Washington knows this. It is not a secret. The politicians' response is simple (simple minds): blame someone else.

Learning how money works includes the idea of creating as many tax-free dollars as you can for your future and your family's future. This is not like guessing in the stock market; this is about planned results. If I were to list three columns in front of you – One Hundred Percent Taxable, Capital Gains Taxable, and a third column, Tax Free – which of the three columns would you want to base the majority of your planning?

In the One Hundred Percent Taxable column are 401Ks, IRAs, pensions, SEPs, and a list of all other qualified retirement plans. In the second column, Capital Gains Taxable, are CDs, mutual funds, stocks, annuities, bank savings, most bonds, etc. The third column, Tax Free, includes family legacies and life insurance. Why does traditional thinking continue to focus on creating more risk and future taxes? Ninety-five percent or all "planning solutions" can be found in the first two columns. Meanwhile, the Tax Free column is, in most cases, not even mentioned. So, in almost all of the discussions about planning today, how can you say yes or no to ideas that a planner doesn't present to you? How can you be aware of an opportunity that isn't explained to you? When it comes to your future, remember these thoughts:

"Did you ever pay a tax you didn't want to? Did you ever pay a tax you didn't have to?" Most of your planning energy should be centered on the tax-free element and opportunities that may be in your life. Learning how money works explores all your financial possibilities. By increasing the tax-free money in your future, you will decrease the amount of taxes you have to pay for the rest of your life. This may be a good time to review Defining Moment #8: Rich people think like rich people; poor people think like poor people.

A Reason to Rejoice –
The Fourth Goal

The amazing opportunity in recapturing transfers and learning how money works is that you can increase your money supply, increase benefits for you and your family, and reduce the amount of risk you face in your life. You can accomplish all of these goals without spending one more dime than you are already spending. Money that you were spending unknowingly and unnecessarily on transfers of your wealth is now yours to keep. Imagine all the possibilities and opportunities that will come your way if you can learn to increase your money supply without having to buy a product, or take more risk in the marketplace. Companies have spent billions of dollars to influence the way you think. You are under constant bombardment by marketing companies who are involved in the transfers of your wealth. Meanwhile, the average American household struggles financially from week to week relying totally on what they have been told to think by these companies who make money peddling their services and products. At the end of the day, and the end of your life, ask yourself one question: What have these companies taught me and did they make more money from me than I made from them?

Ask a typical planner in the financial services business, what is financial planning? You will be amazed by the variety of answers you will get. Some of these answers will be very technical and focused on the products that they sell. Most likely, a real estate person will tell you that the answer to your financial future is real estate. An investment person who sells stocks will tell you the answer is the stock market. A banker may tell you all you need are the bank's CDs. All of their stories will be compelling and filled with almost everything they know and have been trained to know and say (and in some cases what not to say) by their companies. The bigger questions are these: What don't they know? What haven't they been trained to understand? How can they give you the opportunity to say yes or no to ideas that they don't even know exists? So, what really is financial planning? It is wisdom. It is the art form of applying knowledge, logic, and common sense to your everyday life. Knowledge will be the foundation for making better life decisions. Better decisions will help you be more prosperous and create more wealth. All of these results will come from understanding how money works.

The gift of creating more wealth for yourself is inside you. The average person just can't see it. They are too busy just trying to survive or get by, financially. Their lives are out of balance. They spend more time servicing their debt to others than they do on planning their own futures. They have no vision or plan to their lives beyond next week. Worst of all, they have no knowledge of how to help themselves and improve their situations. If you have read this book to this point and studied the Defining Moments, you can no longer be one of these people. You now have the ability to dust off the gift that is already inside you and move forward to improve your life, for the rest of your life.

In learning this process, you may need some help and guidance. It will be important to find a professional who has been through training and will educate and help you improve your life. At the end of this book, I will suggest some guidelines that will help you find the right professional for you.

Defining Moment #10

Understand how money works to live the best life you can live.

Of all the opportunities that you have discovered in your life, which were the most important? Of these opportunities, which ones changed your life forever? Now ask yourself one question: How would the opportunities that you're not even aware of change your life? If you were given one wish, one gift that would fulfill your life, what would it be? Happiness, wealth, health, love – there are many ways you could answer that question. In a very simple way, I would wish to live the best life I could live. Think about that for a second. If given the opportunity, I would like to maximize the gifts I have been given, so I could enjoy my life and share it with others. Your answer to what you want in life may be different from mine, but understand one thing: The gifts and opportunities you have in life are already inside you, but you just can't see them. Discovering these gifts and opportunities is simple. Look for them, and when you find them, learn about them. Your life will change. It's time to live the best life you can live.

There is enough stress, worry, and concern in your everyday life that you may think that changing your life will take a lot of time and energy on your part. But, to change only takes thought and some knowledge. The real truth is that your everyday struggles take up all your time, and you have been enslaved by them. In your financial world the answer to many of your problems is understanding how money works. It isn't fair that throughout your life you have not been given the opportunity and the knowledge to improve your financial life.

Your financial health is centered on much more than simply trying to pick a winning stock or mutual fund. There is no one product that you can purchase that will solve all your financial problems. The solution comes when you understand that everything you own has financial value. When you discover that everything has value, then you can start to understand how you can use your assets as financial tools. These steps will help you create more options and opportunities in your life. Many people are mistaken that the only future dollars they have are their retirement plans and government programs. This is a very narrow approach to the problems you will be facing.

By discovering the Defining Moments, you will develop a thought process that will not only aid you in your everyday financial life but also that will become the foundation of the major decisions you will need to make in planning your financial future. Traditional thinking has put limits on what your thought process can be, and in turn, the outcome will also be limited. The solution to these challenges, the Defining Moments, comes when you understand that everything in your life has value. Future value. When you discover the value of everything you have, then you can start living the best life you can live, right now, today.

In living the best life you can live, you need to view everything in your life as a series of banks, pools of money, that you own and control. With each bank or pool of money, you have the ability to drive the value of your banks higher. Since you own and control all of these banks, you need to make sure all your banks are healthy and well maintained. You need to know how each of your banks work, and also how each bank can work for you. Understanding this will create balance in your financial future. You will then know how to leverage the least amount of money to create the most amount of wealth.

Everything in your life has value and future value. Each one of your banks or pools of money might have different rules. Each one of your banks could have different tax consequences attached to them. All of your banks will have different value and different growth potential. Each one of your banks, or pools of money, will have different exit strategies if you wish to use the money. And, you need to know how to use each one of your banks as financial tools. Most importantly, you need to know how to drive the value of the banks, or money you own, even higher.

If you consider all the value in your life, you may start to rethink your traditional approach. Let's take a look at some values, banks, or pools of money that may already be in your life. The most obvious pools of money that you may already have are the ones you hear about all the time. You may be involved in a qualified plan for your retirement. This type of bank or pool of money could be called a 401K, an IRA, a SEP, or some type of company retirement plan. These types of plans have rules attached to them. Even though they all are retirement programs, some of the rules inside these programs may be different. The rule for these programs that everyone seems to know is that when you retire, the money you receive will be taxed upon withdrawal. The obvious question is this: Will taxes be lower or higher in the future? Unless this is the first page of this book that you're reading, you already know the answer. Another rule of qualified plans is that if you take the money out before retirement or before age 59½, you could face a 10% penalty on the money you take out, on top of having to pay taxes on it. If you understand how money works and you are successful, you must know that retiring to a lower tax bracket is the only way that a qualified retirement plan will work in your favor.

As for the idea of using this pool of money for anything else other than for retirement income has always been viewed as some kind of financial sin. But, you must remember, if one of the deterrents of using this money before you retire is that it will be taxed, the truth is that it will be taxed anyway – now or later. The ten percent penalty is real and is a consideration that should be explored before using retirement money prior to retirement or age 59½. The 10% penalty can be avoided in an IRA if this money is taken out over a lifetime period in equal disbursements according to 72t of the Internal Revenue Code.

The value of your qualified plan will be determined by the results of your investments. Remember, you are the only one at risk in your investment choices. I am not condoning simply cashing in your qualified plans, but you need to understand that this is still your money, and if needed, you can get to it. Breaking the traditional thinking that this pool of money should never be used before retirement is a step to opening doors and opportunities you didn't know existed before.

As a financial tool, qualified plans can play a big role. As a bank or pool of money, you must understand the rules of these programs, understand how and when your money will be taxed, and understand that these programs can be used before and after retirement.

Home Banking

Another financial tool in the average person's life is the value that is inside his home. Traditional thinking has always held that the value of one's home is sacred ground. The changing housing market and potential collapse of real estate values should instill caution in the way anyone purchases and pays for a home. Most of the problems that occur financially in owning a home are created with the purchase of a home, when the buyers fail to realize that taxes and insurance and maintenance costs on this property will continue to increase over the years. But, in most cases, over a period of time, equity will build up in one's home. This can occur in a couple of ways: either the value of the property increases and/or the payments on the house reduces the debt owed, creating equity. Much of the equity in one's home is tax-free money. Learning the rules of this equity is very important. It has value and it is tax-free within the guidelines of the IRS. Equity in your home could act as a bank for you. If the equity is borrowed, it is paid back with interest, but in many cases, the interest that is paid back is tax-deductible. Now, I am not suggesting to take all the money out of your home and invest it. You can see how this pool of money is different from your 401K money and other qualified plans you might have. An interesting question would be: Would you rather have $250,000 in your qualified plan, or $250,000 of equity in your home? Having $250,000 in your qualified plan means you have to pay taxes in order to get it. Having $250,000 of equity in your home means you would have to refinance your house and pay interest in order to get $250,000 of tax-free money. Just imagine if you could trade your taxable qualified plan money for the tax-free money that is inside your home.

The once-taboo idea of using the money that is in your home to live on is now becoming acceptable. Reverse mortgages are back in style. In your retirement years, you could get a reverse mortgage on your home. You could remain in your home for the rest of your life and receive a monthly check or even a lump sum. In exchange, your house belongs to someone else upon your death. Before entering into any agreement of this kind, get a really sharp real estate attorney to assist you. The reason I am discussing reverse mortgage is simply to make you aware that the idea of using the money in your home is not a foreign one.

I have had many discussions with people about families buying the homes of their parents and the parents using the money to increase the value of the legacy that they can leave behind for their children and grandchildren. With proper planning, this legacy would transfer tax-free to the next generation of the family. This would create another pool of money.

The Family Fortune

Many opportunities in life pass you by simply because you weren't aware of them. These opportunities are so critical to your financial future. I feel I have an obligation to share this with you, even if it is to just give you an opportunity to say no to the idea.

The family, your family, may be one of the most powerful financial tools that you have. Traditional thinking neglects to share with you the opportunity that could be created if you were to view your family as an untouched wealth opportunity. You may be surprised to learn that the value of a legacy can be driven higher, wealth can be created, and taxes can be avoided when using your family as a financial tool. I have shared this concept with many readers in my book *The Family Legacy*. I have traveled the country sharing the power of the family legacy with thousands of people. Earlier, we discussed how rich people think like rich people, and poor people think like poor people, in Defining Moment #8. The opportunity of using the family as a tool to create wealth could change your life forever.

Just as your qualified plan money and the money in your home has value, so does the value of your family. Don't allow this conversation about the family to be cast off as uneasy or uncomfortable. Find a qualified professional who is trained in the family legacy to help guide you through the opportunity. You see, how can you say yes or no to ideas you don't even know exist? Just as it is possible to increase the value in your qualified plans and your home, you can also increase the value of your family. The difference is that most of the money from the family can be tax-free. In your qualified plan and the money in your home, you spend and invest a dollar and hope it goes up in value. It is possible that when investing in the family, you can use the least amount of money to create the most amount of wealth. That is what we call leverage.

The New and Old Invest-a-Testament

Another pool of money that many people have is investments in stocks, bonds, and mutual funds. While we are at it, let's include your bank savings also. These investments are different from your qualified plans (IRAs, 401Ks, etc.) when it comes to the rules and taxes. In many cases, your investments, such as stocks and mutual funds, have something in common with your qualified plan: You are the only one at risk. By investing outside of a qualified plan, you shed some of the rules that qualified plans have. Currently, and I mean currently, the tax issues are different in qualified plans, from taxes and capital gains taxes that are paid on most investment gains that you might experience. Qualified plans are taxed at an income tax rate while capital gains tax rates could be a lot lower (check with your tax advisers).

Traditional thinking is of the belief, almost religiously, that investments always go up in value over a period of time. Well, that is true, but not for the reason they want to believe. You see, the stock market must go up because it too reflects inflationary trends. As an example, two thousand years ago, a one-ounce gold coin would buy the average Roman a nice toga, a very nice pair of leather sandals, and a nice leather sash. Today, for the value of one ounce of gold, you can purchase a very nice suit, a nice pair of leather shoes, and a nice leather belt. The value of gold really has not changed over two thousand years, but the value of manmade currency has. The inflationary aspects of our currency appear to drive the value of what we have skyward.

So far, everything that we have talked about in this chapter can be viewed as pools of money that can contribute to future income in your life. As you can see, everything has value and can be used by you to create your best life now.

Bet on Your Life

Another source of money in your life could be your life insurance policy. Professionals of all sorts have opinions, and in most cases, they are only opinions about life insurance and the type of policies people should have. It always cracks me up when I hear someone ranting and raving about the types of policies people should have without knowing anything about the person they are talking to. Just like everything else in life, cheapest may not necessarily be the best. Although the "cheapest" sounds frugal and wise, you wouldn't want to apply that theory to, let's say, your kid's education or to your heart surgeon. There is a time and place where value is important. There are different types of policies that you can purchase, and they all have different rules, values, and results. The most important lesson about life insurance that you should know is this: That life insurance policy you own allows you to spend more of your money now, while you are alive. What I mean by that statement is this: Instead of paying all your debts off as fast as you can, so you can be debt-free, why not buy a policy that will pay off all your debts when you die? If you do this, you can pay off a lifetime of debt for pennies on the dollar and enjoy the life you deserve while you're alive. Think about it: If you could magically create a document that would pay off all your debt at the end of your life, what kind of life would you live now? Many people look at life insurance as a conversation of avoidance, but really, when put in the proper light, it becomes a conversation of opportunity.

The different types of policies out there today have different types of rules, benefits, values, and costs. Term insurance sounds cheap, and if you die, your beneficiary receives tax-free proceeds from that policy. Rule number one here is: You have to die for there to be a benefit for anyone. If you're on a tight budget and can't afford anything else, buy term insurance. The other really important thing you should know is that, by definition, term insurance lasts for only a specific term of time, such as 10, 20, or 30 years, then it expires. If the term policy expires before you do, then there is no benefit and the policy no longer exists.

Buying term insurance at older ages can get very pricey and cost prohibitive.

There is a different set of rules, values, and benefits for cash value life insurance. The first thing you will notice is that it is more expensive, and this is what term insurance sales people emphasize most. But, there is more to cash value life insurance than simply the cost. In these policies, cash value accumulates and grows over a period of time. These values grow tax-deferred. When it comes to the values in these policies, the premiums that you have paid become what is called the *basis* for the values inside them. Let's say you paid, over a number of years, $20,000 in premiums and now the cash value in the policy is $20,000. All of that money is basis and are tax-free values. These policies, if designed right, would have death benefits that increase over the years. Also, if ever needed, these policies can provide tax-free loans to its owner. Cash value policies can also be used as collateral for personal and business loans. The money or values in these types of policies can also be used as a tool for generating additional income in a lump sum or withdrawn on a yearly basis. Remember, these values have some tax-friendly advantages.

It will be up to you when deciding what type of policies you should own. It might be in your best interest to find a highly recommended professional who represents not only term, but also cash value types of policies.

Your policy can become a very valuable tool for you in the future. Rich people know how to use these tools. As I mentioned in an earlier chapter of this book, rich people think like rich people, and the "cheapest" is not always the best.

There's No Business Like Your Business

If you own your own business, you need to understand that your business is a unique opportunity. Not only does your business provide an income for you, but also the opportunity is there to grow and drive forward the value of your business. The secret of owning a business is developing an exit strategy for your business when you decide to retire. Many small businesses simply close their doors when the owner is ready to retire, and with it goes thirty years of experience, goodwill that was built up in that business, and a possible client base. All of these aspects of a business have value. Many business owners fail to see these values and simply shut their business down. Develop a continuation plan for your business after you leave. Your business could be a great investment for someone else, and create more future dollars for you. Like everything else in life, more time and energy should be spent on exploring the exit strategies for our lives.

The Money Matrix

To understand how money works, you need to apply a litmus test to measure the effectiveness and usefulness of your money. It is important to remember that way too much emphasis is put on the "rate of return" mentality and too little on how money can work for you. The litmus test for money contains a series of questions that will define the most effective types of money that you currently have, and guide you towards other types of money that you might want to have.

There are a number of categories that the money you have right now may fall into. You can have IRAs, 401Ks, Roth IRAs, defined benefit programs, SEPs, mutual funds, bank savings programs, CDs, stocks, your home, real estate, your business, possible inheritances, and life insurance. You may be able to think of more, but these are the most general categories of money that you might have. If you take each one of these categories and list them in a column, and ask the following questions of each one of your money categories, you will discover the efficiency, effectiveness, and safety of the money you have.

The Questions

RISK: DOES THIS CATEGORY OR TYPE OF MONEY INVOLVE RISK? Can you lose your money? As an example, can your 401K lose money? Can your home lose value? Are mutual funds and stocks subject to losses? Can your bank saving program lose money? There are different degrees of risk. Some things may be more risky than others, so when it comes to each of your categories, mark each one "H" for high risk, "M" for medium risk, or "L" for low risk. If this category or type of money has no risk, write "NONE." Ask the risk question of all the types of money you have.

Next Question. . .

GUARANTEES: DOES THIS CATEGORY OR TYPE OF MONEY OFFER GUARANTEES? Is this category or type of money assuring you of a controlled positive result in the future? Some guarantees may have a stipulation attached to them, like keeping your money in an account for a certain number of years. Does an IRA have guarantees? Does the money or equity in your home have guarantees? Does that mutual fund you own have guarantees? For every type of money that you have, simply answer: yes or no.

Next Question. . .

PENALTIES: DOES THIS CATEGORY OR TYPE OF MONEY HAVE PENALTIES ASSOCIATED WITH IT? This question is an important one that you must understand. Many types of your money might have penalties attached to them. An example may be: Are there penalties for early withdrawal of an IRA? Are there penalties for not taking enough money out of your IRA during retirement? Are there early withdrawal penalties for a bank CD? How about a penalty for paying your house off too soon? Are there any penalties in annuities or back-loaded mutual funds? For each category or type of money, simply write yes or no if penalties exist.

Next Question. . .

LIQUIDITY, USE, AND CONTROL: DOES THIS CATEGORY OR TYPE OF MONEY GIVE YOU THE OPPORTUNITY TO GET TO YOUR MONEY IF YOU NEED IT? Do you have access to your money? Can you get it when you need it? Answering simply yes or no will give you a clearer view of whether you control this type or category of money. Do you have an equity line of credit on your business or your home? Can you sell off your stocks and mutual funds? If money is quickly needed, what type or category of money would you turn to? So, do you have liquidity, use, and control of this type of money, yes or no?

Next Question. . .

PROTECTED: IS THIS CATEGORY OR TYPE OF MONEY PROTECTED FROM CREDITORS? If you were to get sued, what types of money would be protected against lawsuits? Money you have in the bank? The equity in your home? Your investments? Your 401K? This is important to know. Many people are at great risk and don't even know it. Simply answer yes or no to all of the types of your money that may be exposed to lawsuits.

Next Question. . .

LEVERAGE: DOES THIS CATEGORY OR TYPE OF MONEY USE LEVERAGE? Does this type of money create the most amount of money for the least amount you invest? We discussed leverage earlier in this book. When someone invests a dollar, the hope is that dollar will grow over a period of time. It doesn't create increased value or increased net worth the next day. Simply compounding the value of a dollar may also increase or compound the taxes due on it. The thought of leverage is not typically centered on rates of return but more on controlling and creating wealth or value. As an example, if you had $200,000 in the bank today that would be good. The next day you bought a $500,000 home and put the $200,000 down as a down payment. So, in a day, you went from doing well with $200,000 in the bank, to being $300,000 in debt. Did this person leverage the least amount of money to purchase this home, or leverage the most amount of money? What's the rate of return on the $200,000 of equity in this new home? Why, it's zero. You might be thinking your monthly payment will be lower and it would be, but you also lost the time value of the $200,000, as well as what it could grow to in value. Once again, Donald Trump would not put the most amount of money down on a piece of property; he would leverage the least amount of money to gain control of the property. Another example of leverage would be someone whose net worth is one million dollars today, and the next day he bought a million dollar life insurance policy for one hundred dollars a month. His life value doubled in one day for $100 per month. Leverage. . . it can create wealth. Are you using the least amount of money to create the most amount of wealth?

Next Question. . .

TAX-DEFERRED: DOES THIS TYPE OR CATEGORY OF MONEY GROW TAX-DEFERRED? Very few things in our lives escape taxation. Many types of money are taxed on their growth on an annual basis. A typical CD at a bank is taxed on its growth on an annual basis. Is this true of an IRA or 401K? No, these are tax-deferred. These are taxed when you take distributions from them. So, the tax on them is deferred to a later date and possibly a higher tax table. Ask yourself, does your money or a particular type of money grow tax-deferred? Yes or no.

Next Question. . .

TAX-FREE: DOES THIS TYPE OF MONEY GET DISTRIBUTED TO YOU TAX-FREE? Better yet, does the type of money you have get distributed to you or your heirs, your family, in the event of something happening to you, tax-free? Is an IRA tax-free? How about a bank savings program? Are mutual funds tax-free? On your chart or list of types of money you can have, how many of them are tax-free at distribution? Yes or no.

Next Question. . .

COLLATERAL: CAN THIS TYPE OR CATEGORY OF MONEY BE USED AS COLLATERAL FOR LOANS? Sometimes lending institutions will grant loans if there is some type of collateral or hard asset involved. A home could be used as collateral for a loan but how about an IRA or a 401K? Can mutual funds be used as collateral? Collateral typically has value that is relatively safe and assures a lending institution of controlling value while lending your money. If money was needed by you or your family, what assets do you control that could be used for collateral? What assets or types of money could be used to get a loan that could increase the value of, let's say, your business? Do the types of money you have provide value to anyone else? Think about it. . . yes or no.

Next Question. . .

TAX-DEDUCTIBLE PAYMENTS: ARE THE PAYMENTS FOR THIS TYPE OF MONEY TAX-DEDUCTIBLE ON YOUR INCOME TAXES? Some types of money are tax-deductible from your income. Within the guidelines of the IRS, payments to 401Ks and IRAs are tax-deductible. How about a typical mutual fund investment – is that tax-deductible? How about an annuity or a bank CD? Interest payments on some types of money are also tax-deductible. A principle payment on your home is not tax-deductible, but the interest portion of that payment is. Try to think if any other types of your money have tax-deductible payments. Yes or no?

Next Question. . .

DISABILITY BENEFIT: IN THE EVENT OF AN ILLNESS OR ACCIDENT IN YOUR LIFE, WILL THIS TYPE OR CATEGORY OF MONEY CONTINUE TO MAKE DEPOSITS OR PAYMENTS FOR YOU WHILE YOU'RE DISABLED? Will your company continue to make your 401K deposits for you even if you're not working? Will your investment broker continue to make monthly payments or deposits into your account for you while you were injured or sick? Would the bank make your mortgage payment? What types of money do you own that would make the payment for you if you were disabled? Will the company you're dealing with deposit or make the payment for this type of money? Yes or no.

Next Question. . .

WEALTH TRANSFERS: WILL THIS TYPE OR CATEGORY OF MONEY TRANSFER TO YOUR HEIRS TAX-FREE? In the event of your death, how will the type of money you have be taxed or transferred to the next generation of family members or heirs? Will someone else have to pay the tax on your IRA if you die? How about your mutual funds or bank CDs? Does the government forgive the taxes on the investment you left behind? Does this type of money you have create real tax-free wealth for your family, kids, or heirs? Apply this question to all the types of your money. Simply answer yes or no.

Your Answers

Your answers to these questions could be very eye opening when it comes to how your money works. If you had the ability to create the perfect investment for yourself, how would these questions be answered? Would there be a lot of risk involved? Would there be some guarantees? Would you create an investment where there would be penalties? Would you like liquidity, use, and control of your money? Would you protect it from creditors? Would your perfect investment create leverage? Would it grow tax-deferred? Would you make it tax-free when you decided to use the money? Would you design it so that it can be used as collateral to secure loans? Would the money you put into it be tax-deductible? Would there be a disability benefit on the payments? Finally, would the money you have transfer tax-free to your heirs?

You will discover, when creating the most perfect investment, that the answers you gave are far different from the money and investments you have right now. The types of money that you have are far from perfect. Remember, there are only three types of categories that your money falls into: lifestyle, accumulated, and transferred money. One final question you should ask yourself: If given a choice, would you want your money to be fully taxed, partially taxed, or tax-free? While this question really answers itself, why is it that we ignore what is logical and expose most of our saving and investing efforts to full or partial taxation?

By listing the types of money that you have and asking the important questions that we just discussed, you will get a clearer view of the money that is in your life and how it works. The money matrix measures each type of money that you may have by:

RISK
GUARANTEES
PENALTIES
LIQUIDITY, USE, AND CONTROL
PROTECTION
LEVERAGE
TAX DEFERRAL
TAX DISTRIBUTION
COLLATERAL
PAYMENTS
DISABILITY CONTINUATION
WEALTH TRANSFER

Of the twelve measurements, a typical mutual fund might have only three or four favorable outcomes for an individual. Today, mutual funds remain one of the largest sectors for investing. Remember your answers, if you could design the perfect investment, and now compare them with mutual funds. You may discover mutual funds missed your criteria as a favorable investment eight or nine out of twelve times. This is not to say that mutual funds are bad but to shine some light on what we have, compared to what we want.

Your Approach

Everything you do in life and the results of your actions will depend upon how you prepare. If you wanted to become a doctor, you wouldn't prepare for this career by studying all the art courses you could in college, unless of course you were interested in having the fanciest waiting room in the world. To be a doctor, you would study all the appropriate courses and then enter into medical school.

Your money is no different. You need to apply a thought process to where you want to be in your financial future. Heading into that future without a clue of how your money will support you will expose you to too many unintended consequences. Now is the time to understand how your money works and all the opportunities that might be right in front of you. The defining moment in your life will occur when you are no longer "out of control" in your financial life.

The information in this book will help you analyze your financial situation and help give you a clearer view of the choices open to you and will help you make better life decisions in the future.

Why Traditional Thinking Fails to Meet Its Goals

It is my opinion that in order to improve our lives I believe it is necessary to enlist a new thought process. The ten "defining moments" is a simple yet effective thought process that was designed to help you analyze your current situation and help create more options and opportunities in your life.

Many people are finding it difficult to get ahead in today's financial world. I would like to share with you why I feel "getting ahead" and meeting life's financial goals remain elusive to many. The reality is that right from the beginning, the deck is stacked against you.

I am not going to blame all the professionals in the financial services industry, as there are many highly trained professionals out there. Some are better than others. Their job is very difficult because, whether they understand it or not, the deck is also stacked against them. If you need the services of a professional, you might be better off working with one who can explain the challenges that both of you face. Traditional planning and thinking is not a science. If it were, no one would lose money. I feel it is far more important to use a common sense and logical approach in the attempt to secure your financial future. Even then, it will be difficult to achieve your goals. You have to take a much deeper look at why this is such an elusive challenge.

Theories & Factors

Traditional thinking is mired in the thought that accumulation and rates of return are two factors that will determine your future success. Although on the surface these factors seem important, they will not secure or determine future success. As I have discussed throughout this book, I believe it is far more important to understand how your money works and the buying power of your dollar, and then, you can more effectively and efficiently use your money.

The Accumulation Factor

I believe that accumulating a lot of money is a good thing. Traditional thinking will establish goals of how many dollars you will need in the future to secure your financial success. Reaching accumulation goals are seldom achieved, which is not your fault or the fault of the planner. Here is why these goals are difficult to achieve.

The reality is that we live in a country that has a "flexible currency." Our currency is created by the Federal Reserve (the banks) and distributed by the Federal Government. The dollar in its creation has no real value. That means it is not backed by silver or gold that would give it value. The flaw in the flexible currency design is that it automatically creates an inflation factor. If the currency had real value from the start, there would be very little, if any, inflation. It is almost impossible to nail down the value and buying power of flexible currency at any time in the future. Simply planning to reach an accumulation level in the future is good, but achieving this may fall far short of your buying power expectations in the future.

The accumulation factor also offers you some guarantees. FIRST, in trying to accumulate and make your money grow...you are the only one at risk. SECOND, that growth will probably be taxed. At what level it will be taxed is anyone's guess. So, the accumulation factor has a lot of moving parts, such as the flexible currency, its future buying power, risk in the marketplace, and taxes, along with the threat of even higher taxes in the future.

In the accumulation factor, the central thought is the more money you have, the better it is. But, with all the hurdles, reaching fulfillment in this type of thinking is challenging. It is like a basketball coach telling his players that they better go out and score 200 points in the game because they have no defense in the challenges they face.

The Rate of Return Factor

Another reason why traditional thinking and planning falls short of its goals is the rate of return factor. People are of the belief that if they can grow their money at a certain rate of return then all will be well in the future. Rates of return have been used by planners as a barometer of how you are doing over a period of time. They also use past performance rates of return as if they were some indication of the future. Although past performance is some indication of stability, management, and success, it really offers only a glimmer of possible performance in the future. When you buy an investment, your performance history starts that day, not ten years ago.

Rates of return are a performance measurement. The reality is that you cannot spend rates of return; you can only spend money. Rates of return can be misleading and confusing when used for a measurement of your success. Everyone looks for that positive rate of return, but those returns create a false sense of security.

What You See and What You Get

As an example, let's take a look at a homeowner who bought a house nine years ago for $175,000. Over that period of nine years, the value of the house rose to $250,000. The owner of the home looks at this growth and says, "WOW, that is more than a 40% increase." Although that statement is true, I wouldn't go out and buy that "I'm A Genius" t-shirt yet. The reality is that when you take into consideration the time frame of nine years, the real rate of return is 4.04% per year.

Another example of what you see and what you get will alarm you. In a time frame from 2000 through 2007, the Dow Industrial averaged 2.57%. That is the average of the average. Using that average for those eight years, one could assume that if he had invested $100,000 and received the average 2.57% rate of return, he would have accumulated $122,495.60. But...if a person had actually been in the market every year for those eight years and received the Dow's actual return, he would only have achieved a 1.80% rate of return, not 2.57%. He would have accumulated $115,379.39. That is about 40% less than what the proclaimed eight-year average was.

When doing future assumptions, and using a constant average rate of return, the assumption and what you get may be totally different.

Rates of return are flexible and unpredictable in the future. Rates of return are a measuring stick. Like a thermometer, it can tell you your body temperature and can serve as a warning that you may be coming down with a cold or the flu; however, it doesn't indicate specific serious conditions you may have.

Just as the accumulation factor, the rate of return factor has many variables and moving parts. Traditional thinking cannot control and predict a future outcome of all these variables successfully.

The Taxation Factor

The taxation factor is unique because we know it is going to impact us now and in the future, but we just don't know to what extent. Realizing that a 15% to 40% guaranteed loss factor due to taxation looms in our future is a serious consideration that should not be ignored.

Our government tax policy is flexible (another moving part). It can go up and down, depending upon your success. Not only are our income and savings taxed, but also the government has created layers and layers of non-income and growth taxes. A phone bill may have two or three taxes on it. Your cable bill, staying at a hotel, purchasing an airline ticket, the gas that you pump into your car – all have two, three, or more associated taxes. The government taxes businesses and the businesses simply pass on their taxation cost to the consumer, you and me, in the form of higher prices. Overall, tax rates have grown over 40% faster than our incomes over the last 20 years.

Many times in using accumulation and rate of return planning and thinking, the marketing and selling of these concepts and products gloss over the taxation factor. Once again, the taxation factor has many moving parts that are unpredictable, as are the accumulation and rate of return factors.

The Market Factor

The market factor is really pretty simple. An average person on his way home from work or at the end of the day is likely to hear how the market performed for that day. The Dow was up 50 points or the Dow was down 35 points; the S&P 500 was up or possibly down; the NASDAQ had a good day or bad day, etc. With that 10 seconds of information, the average person assesses that information into two categories: that all is good or oh well. The reality is that the markets are measured on volume, numbers of trades, and the value of the trades (this is the simple explanation). The fact that the market went up or down has no bearing on the buying power that you control. The market indicators are a daily flexible measuring stick whose movement, if you choose to, can be watched by the second on television or websites. If you are making decisions based on market returns, you are betting that because it has done well in the past, it will continue to do so (Enron, WorldCom, Fannie Mae, The Airline Industry) into the future. The hope is that the average person is smart enough, or should be, to understand that the slot machine that he is playing has paid off three times in a row, and will continue to win, right? No.

There are professionals who play the market game very well and they know their stuff, but even they cannot control the trends and flexibility of the markets. These professionals do not use past performances of a company to determine whether to invest in them or not. They use information based on the future opportunities that these companies have that will increase their revenues and earnings. The problem is by the time most of this good information gets to the public, you and me, a lot of the opportunity in gaining value is already gone. If you are a hunter, it is like shooting where the duck was.

The daily market results and averages should not be the sole foundation for your financial strategies. I believe you must first have knowledge of how your money works and understand the buying power of your dollar. Knowing how money works in your life will help you maximize your money supply, create leverage for your future dollars, and eliminate many of the flexible pitfalls that come with traditional thinking. Learn to think for yourself instead of being told what to think.

The Human Factor

Let's face it: No amount of planning will ever prevent dumb luck. Unfortunately, many people are involved in "Poverty Planning." Poverty planning takes no time, no money, and the results are pretty predictable. There is a reason why people are stuck in this mode: They have had little or no success with planning; they feel they are not knowledgeable, and/or they are embarrassed to discuss their situation with anyone. They avoid and delay and simply hope that things will turn out okay. For some Americans, surviving and living week to week is difficult. Confusion and embarrassment aside, frustration is totally understandable, and the information and knowledge discussed in this book could give you a defining moment in your life.

The other part of the human factor is consistency. Many people, after suffering losses or continuing to follow losing strategies, just give up. Some professionals do not know what they should know, and many people do not know much at all when it comes to the financial world. These two ingredients are a dangerous combination in trying to produce positive results.

Moving Flexible Parts

I hope you now have a better understanding of what is happening in your life. With all the moving and flexible possibilities in traditional thinking and with all the possible variables and outcomes of the accumulation factor, rate of return factor, the taxation factor, the market factor, and the human factor, you may have discovered why traditional planning and thinking fails to meet its goals. Any effort or attempt to plan for the future should be applauded, misguided as it may be. With more information, you will be able to make better decisions. A new thought process will be your defining moment. I do believe some planning in your life, as confusing as it can get, is better than no planning. I also believe that what you know and understand today will shape your tomorrow, not only for you but also for the next generation. Seek out a professional who understands the defining moments, and that will help you live the best life you can today!

A Professional Profile

Learning how your money works will result in a defining moment, but in many cases, you may need support and assistance when it comes to planning and fully understanding a sound financial thought process. Finding a competent professional to help you is sometimes difficult. Many professionals have the misfortune of not knowing what they should know. Traditional thinking will result in traditional results, and this is not good enough in today's financial world. It will be important to find a professional who has been exposed to the understanding of how money works. If a professional has forwarded this book to you, then he (she) is aware of the value of its content. He may be the professional that is willing to take the time to educate you and teach you how money works. Seek out experience and knowledge from a professional that does more than push financial products. You need to create a long-standing relationship with a professional whose standards are high. Many professionals have taken the time and have been exposed to the thought process we have discussed. It has become a valuable tool for them with tremendous results for their clients and, potentially, for you.

Other books that I have written may deepen your understanding of how money works: *Learning to Avoid Unintended Consequences*, *Sudden Impact*, and *The Family Legacy*, published by Infinity Publishing. Many professionals have used these books because they too are concerned about the direction we are heading as a country and the impact it will have on everyone's financial future. You see, how can you be aware of something you're not aware of, and how can you say yes or no to ideas that you don't even know exist?